The Kennebec River

The Kennebec River

by Louise Dickinson Rich

illustrated by Lili Réthi, (F.R.S.A.)

HOLT, RINEHART AND WINSTON

NEW YORK   CHICAGO   SAN FRANCISCO

Contents

WHAT IS A RIVER? • 9

RED CLAY AND OYSTER SHELLS • 13

THE DAWN PEOPLE • 17

THE FIRST WHITE MEN • 25

CUSHNOC • 36

GOD'S WORD ON THE KENNEBEC • 42

THE TIME OF TERROR • 47

ARNOLD'S MARCH TO QUEBEC • 58

MR. MADISON'S WAR • 64

THE BOY FROM SCARBORO • 74

KING LOG • 78

THE CIVIL WAR • 84

KENNEBEC CRYSTALS • 91

NO PRICE ATTACHED • 97

THE KENNEBEC TODAY • 108

INDEX • 119

The Kennebec River

WHAT IS A RIVER?

Because human life originated and flourished along their banks, rivers have been likened to cradles. The valley of the Tigris and Euphrates, for instance, has been called the cradle of Babylonian culture. Rivers have been compared to highways along which explorers and settlers could travel into unknown, distant areas. The Mississippi is a good example of this. Rivers such as the Rio Grande serve as barriers and boundaries separating nations; or a river like the Nile may bind the people of a country together, may be the backbone that supports a civilization.

Some rivers, like the Ganges, have been regarded as sacred objects of worship. Others have been used as symbols, so that dying is sometimes poetically referred to as "crossing the River Jordan." Rivers have often been bones of contention. No matter what other complicated excuses for fighting may be given, many wars boil down to quarrels over the control of a river basin like that of the Saar.

It would be impossible to erase the mention of rivers from any history, because it would be impossible for life, whether plant or animal, to exist on earth without them. Rivers are the veins and arteries of the world.

The Kennebec, by ordinary standards, is not a very big river. It is only 164 miles long, and nowhere very wide or very deep. It begins at Moosehead, Maine's largest lake in the heart of the hills, and runs due south. At Merrymeeting Bay it is joined by its chief tributary, the 175-mile Androscoggin, and the two go out through a fine lacework of coastal islands into the Atlantic. Together the Androscoggin and the Kennebec—which the Indians called the Quinnebequi, the River God—drain more than half of Maine. Their countless brooks, creeks, and ponds lie like a silver web over the whole central part of the state. Within this shining network are forests and farmlands, cities, towns, and tiny hamlets. Yet the whole thing covers comparatively little territory. Maine is one of the smallest states in the Union, and nothing within it is truly enormous except the loyalty and pride of its sons and daughters.

Why, then, is the Kennebec one of the great rivers of the world, greater perhaps than the Amazon, the longest on earth? What makes a river great?

A river is as great as its influence on history and its service to mankind. The little Kennebec has been almost everything that it is possible for a river to be. It was the cradle for a whole breed of remarkable men—the early American pioneers who were hunters, fishermen, farmers, investors, sailors, and lumbermen rolled into one. The descendants of these men opened up the West, taking their Down East ingenuity, individuality, and wry Yankee humor to Ohio, Michigan, Wisconsin, Minnesota, and across the Rockies to Oregon and Washington.

The Kennebec was at times a boundary between the territories claimed in early days by the French and the English. It was worshiped as a god by some of the Indian tribes. It has watered crops and turned the wheels of mills and factories. Frozen into crystal blocks, its water has cooled parched throats in faraway tropic lands. It has been a vast shipyard and a clear road into the wilderness. It has, like a conveyor-belt, carried millions of pine logs from the inaccessible mountains to the waiting ships of lumber-hungry countries overseas. Wars have been fought because of it, and whole ways of living determined by its nature. And it has been very much loved by those who have known it.

The Kennebec is indeed a great river.

CANADA

MT. KATAHDIN

MOOSEHEAD LAKE

Carratunk

Kennebec River

Skowhegan

Norridgewock

Androscoggin R.

SNOW
FALLS

Little Androscoggin R.

Augusta

MAINE

NEW HAMPSHIRE

SABBATHDAY
LAKE

Topsham
Brunswick

Wiscasset
Edgecomb
Bath
Arrowsic

Popham

ATLANTIC OCEAN

One
RED CLAY AND OYSTER SHELLS

The first settlers on the banks of the Kennebec were Stone Age men. These were very likely descendants of the prehistoric forest dwellers of France and Spain. Eons ago, much of the Northern Hemisphere was covered by a gigantic icecap. As the great glacier melted and retreated toward the Pole, the tribes living along its edge followed, gradually spreading over Asia. Around 3000 B.C. they reached and crossed over the Bering Straits. Eight or nine centuries later, they finally arrived at the Atlantic coast and the Kennebec valley.

They brought with them on their long journey through time and space some of their skills and some of their folkways. They employed the bow and arrow, the trap, and the pitfall. They knew about fire and its use. They had not yet learned to gather, sow, and reap wild seeds, or that wild sheep and goats could be domesticated; but they did have dogs very much like small huskies which they used for hunting and as watchdogs, and enjoyed as pets and companions.

Their life in the beautiful valley is easy to imagine. They hunted and fished, as primitive tribes everywhere have always done, dug oysters and clams, and speared salmon in the river. In summer they picked the blueberries, raspberries, and blackberries that grew in hot, windless clearings; and in the fall sniffed the winey, frost-tinged Maine air and marveled at the autumn foliage—gold, orange, scarlet, and deep crimson—blazing on the hillsides. They must have gazed in awe at the Northern Lights—the aurora borealis—crackling up from the horizon in streamers a hundred miles long; and moved like ghosts through the thick fogs that drift down on occasion from the Bay of Fundy. In winter they huddled beneath the lash of a knife-edged blizzard and, when the storm was over, dug themselves out into a world of dazzling white overarched by a sky unbelievably blue. They must have taken heart when the sun climbed higher, day by day, and the snows shrank until at last green grass and yellow dandelions appeared.

In short, they lived as all men since have lived in the valley. They worked and played, loved and hated, grieved and rejoiced, aware always of the world around them and the river flowing past their doors.

They had a sense of beauty. This we know through the few things that have been found in graves at Carratunk and other places. The ancient bones crumble to dust at the first breath of air, but the stone artifacts have endured. There are flint arrowheads as delicately sculptured as the petals of a daisy, and skinning knives hollow-ground to the keenest possible edge. While hunting, they used weighted rawhides which they threw to entangle the legs of deer. The thongs have long since disappeared, but the stone weights remain. They are exquisitely shaped and proportioned, and their sides are carved with flowers of great elegance. When these people ran through the forest, they wore necklaces of blue stones, shaped into crescents and beautifully carved. They liked nice things.

This lost race is sometimes called the Red Clay people, because mingled with the dust of their graves there is always found clay stained red with iron oxide. This, too, was a practice brought from Europe, where similar red-lined graves are found. Scientists have determined the source of the iron oxide: a pit on the slope of

14

Katahdin, at a great distance from some of the graves in which it appears. They do not know, though, whether this color was used for decorating the body, in an attempt to embalm the dead, or as part of some religious ritual. They only know that it was important enough to make the long trek to Katahdin necessary.

The Red Clay people were followed by another lost race, the Oyster Shell men, the tribe that left enormous heaps of oyster shells along the entire Maine coast. Some of them rise as high as twenty-five feet, and one contains an estimated forty-five million cubic feet of empty oyster shells. This represents a lot of oysters eaten.

The Oyster Shell men, of course, did not live on oysters alone. They ate fish, game, wild fowl, berries, and fruit as well. But at certain seasons they traveled from their valley homes to the coastal oyster beds. The shell heaps mark the locations of these tribal outings. Sometimes artifacts and even bones are found near them. These provide clues to the lives and natures of the people who feasted there.

The bones suggest that these people were big, standing over six feet tall. There is no telling how they died, because the bones crumble before any close examination can be made.

More interesting than these slightly ghoulish relics are the things that were broken or lost during the excitement of the picnic. There are crude copper spoons, bits of rough pottery decorated with comb markings, primitive axes and knives, arrow and spear heads, bone combs and needles. Evidently these excursions to the oyster beds took days or even weeks, and the people came prepared. They brought not only cooking utensils, but sewing kits, toilet articles, and probably other emergency items as well.

These affairs must really have been fun. Looking at the age-old ashes of a cooking fire amid the bleached shells, you can picture how it was. The light of the fire leaped and wavered on the dark wall of the forest behind and the softly flowing water below. Around it sat the Oyster Shell families, reaching for oysters, eating them with gusto, tossing shells over shoulders, reaching for more. Then, full at last, they went about the camp chores—putting children to bed, feeding the dogs, mending torn clothing, restringing bows and chipping out new arrowheads, talking and laughing and playing jokes on each other. They were people like us, and must have behaved about as we do when we feel free and happy and in holiday mood.

But they are all gone and forgotten now, lost in the mists of prehistory.

Two THE DAWN PEOPLE

When the first Europeans sailed into the mouth of the Kennebec, they were watched from the shadows of the forest by a people quite different from the Red Clay and Oyster Shell men. These were the lean and handsome Abenakis, who called themselves the Dawn People.

Unlike the earlier inhabitants of the valley, the Abenakis were primarily farmers. As farmers do everywhere in the world, they hunted, fished, and trapped and they could, when necessary, be tough, resourceful fighters. But their real concern was the little plots of squash, corn, beans, and pumpkins planted between the rocks and stumps of their scrubby acres. They cultivated these gardens with clamshell hoes, spades of wood or moose horn, and rakes made by shredding and binding with bark fiber the ends of saplings. They fertilized their crops by planting with them herring and shad, which they called *menhaden*, meaning "they manure." In some parts of Maine these fish are still known as *menhaden*.

Knowing from experience that a Kennebec winter is a long, cold, starving-time, the Indians dried as much of their harvest as possible and stored it in holes in the ground or in houses of bark and skin. In summer they picked and dried wild grapes and berries, and in autumn gathered nuts and edible roots. Their summer surplus of fish and game they smoked or dried against a time of need. Even in the worst winters, when the game disappeared, the streams were frozen almost solid, and the whole world was encased in ice and snow, they did not go hungry.

Nor did they develop scurvy, a disease caused by a lack of vitamins and common over much of the world at the time. Knowing nothing about vitamins, the Indians nevertheless managed a well-balanced diet. With their meat, fruit, vegetables, and cornbread, they drank quantities of a tea made by steeping spruce tips, an excellent vitamin source. In the spring they sought out fresh greens—dandelions, goose grass, and the fern fronds called fiddleheads. They tapped the maple trees, collected the sap, and drank it as a spring tonic. What was left over they boiled down into syrup and sugar. Although they lacked some things that we consider almost necessary—coffee, butter, milk, and potatoes, for example —their fare was much better than adequate. The early white settlers were smart enough to adopt these Indian practices to their own advantage.

Kennebec Valley farmers today work the same acres that the Abenakis opened to the sun. In the spring they dig dandelion greens, hunt for fiddleheads, and tap the maple trees. They walk to their woodlots in winter on snowshoes, use bayberry candles when the power fails in a storm, and find comfort in a good pipeful of tobacco. These things, too, are legacies of the Dawn People of a thousand years ago.

Prehistoric man was free to roam wherever he wished. The Abenakis were not. Their farms were not much by modern standards, but they had put into them too much backbreaking labor with their primitive tools to go off and leave them to coons, deer, weeds, and the encroaching forest. So their villages were permanent. The houses were built of timber and roofed with bark or thatch. A hole at the peak let out most of the smoke from the fire kept burning in a central fireplace for cooking and heat. For added warmth in winter, the foundations were banked with sod, leaves,

An Indian village.

and branches, a custom still common along the Kennebec.

In summer, between planting and harvest when the gardens needed little care, the villages were almost deserted for a week or two. Only a handful of men too old for travel remained as watchmen. The rest of the tribe went to the seashore to fish and gather clams, oysters, and lobsters. It was their vacation.

They traveled light. They took fire, of course, slow-burning punk placed between two large clam shells and encased thickly in wet clay. They left their heavy pottery bowls at home and took instead beautifully made baskets, tight enough to hold water. Light and convenient, these baskets served as luggage on the trip. Then, emptied of their contents, they became cooking pots. They were filled with water which was brought to a boil by dropping red-hot stones into it. Add a few handfuls of ground corn, and there was a nourishing bowl of cornmeal mush for breakfast; or throw in a few lobsters and ears of green corn, and there was a dinner fit for a king.

There was a free, careless feeling about these excursions. Only necessary work was done around the camp, only light and airy shelters of brush and poles were erected. Most of the time was spent in swimming, fishing, wrestling, racing, jumping, and playing intricate ball games on the shining sand or singing shingle. The old Abenakis knew that the good time could not last forever. All the while, weeds were growing in the vegetable plots back home, and woods mice and porcupines were preparing to move into the empty lodges. Soon it would be time to go home and again take up the serious business of living. So they made the most of the short interlude.

If ever the Dawn People had a friend among the forest trees, it was the lovely white birch. They used large pieces of the bark, sewn together with root fibers, sealed with pitch, and stretched over light wooden frames, to make canoes. Some of these craft were large enough to hold twenty-five or thirty persons and seaworthy enough to make possible long journeys through rough seas to the faraway coastal island called Monhegan. Some were small enough to be handled easily by one man through the rapids to the upper reaches of the Kennebec. The Old Town canoe, considered the best-designed canoe in the world, is modeled exactly on the old birch-bark canoe of the Abenakis, although different, modern materials are used in its construction.

There were other uses of the birch. Light, strong toboggans for hauling game or freight over deep snows were made of bark fastened to thin laths. Boxes, bowls, and buckets were fashioned of tightly sewn bark. The delicate, rose-colored inner bark was used as paper on which to record historic events, treaties, and messages in the written symbols that the Abenakis had invented. Birch poles were used to frame houses and as handles for tools. Scraps of bark were used to kindle fires; and the wood, which split easily even under the crude Indian axes of stone, was a principal firewood.

The live birch, so lithe and limber, was used for setting snares. The top of the tree, equipped with a rawhide noose and a triggering device, was bent down and lightly secured to the ground along a game trail. Nudged by an unsuspecting victim, the tree sprang up, carrying a rabbit, a fox, a deer, or even a bear or moose with it to dangle aloft until the trapper came along.

The same strong flexibility gave the Indian children a piece of playground apparatus. They would climb to the top of the tree, hugging the trunk to preserve the delicate balance. Then, gripping tight with their hands, they launched into space. The birch set

Monhegan Island.

them down gently on the earth and, with a soft, leafy swishing, rushed upward again.

Men along the Kennebec today split birch for firewood and save the bark for kindling. They make little cups, which they leave beside springs in the forest, out of circles of birch bark folded over and pinned with twigs. They whittle out axe handles from the straight-grained wood. And Kennebec children still swing birches, just as Abenaki children did.

Any people who live close to nature develop a religion. They cannot observe the rotation of the seasons, the march of the sun, moon, and stars through the heavens, the coming and going of the tides, without wondering who is behind this orderly plan. The Dawn People believed that the planner was a Spirit who lived up near where the Kennebec began, among the peaks of Katahdin. They kept away from the mountain as much as possible. The Spirit did not like intruders. If a man went too close, there would come a rushing and a roaring. When it was over, the man would have disappeared. We may smile and mention snowslides and avalanches; but even today people unaccountably disappear on Katahdin. The Abenakis were right in treating the brooding mountain with respect.

The Dawn People, like other American Indians, practiced a democratic form of government. Romantic stories are told of beautiful Indian princesses, but the fact is that the Indians had no royalty. Each tribe was governed by two chiefs, a war chief and a peace chief. It is easy to see why. The wise, temperate older men who could settle village disputes would not have the fierce, ruthless nature or the physical strength necessary for leadership in battle. These chiefs or sagamores were elected by the people and served as long as they did their jobs well, and no longer. No

23

chief acted alone. Each was advised and assisted in his job by a tribal council of respected men.

Twice a year, in October and in April, council meetings were held, usually on an island set aside for the purpose. Anyone who had a grievance could air it. The sagamores then consulted together and delivered their judgment. That ended the matter. Nobody disputed the council's decisions.

Actually, it was not too hard to keep the peace among the members of a tribe. A great many modern lawsuits arise over real estate. An Abenaki owned personal property such as clothes, weapons, and household goods; but nobody owned any land. Deeds of sale and transfer of real property were unknown. All outdoors—the woods, fields, shore and riverbanks—was common property. No Indian would be able to imagine saying, "This plot belongs to me, and you keep off it." This approach prevented a great deal of ill-feeling.

That approach was also to be the cause of almost a hundred years of bloodshed, screams of agony in the night, and countless English homesteads and hamlets wrapped in flame. For the quiet, peaceable, hard-working and hard-playing Dawn People who watched the first European ships sail into the Kennebec were to change. Then they had been simply curious and perhaps a little shy. Later they were to become suspicious and wary of these men who did not seem able to understand the laws of their world. And finally they realized that their way of life and their very lives were at stake, and they acted accordingly.

Three THE FIRST WHITE MEN

The first Europeans to sail among the lovely islands at the mouth of the Kennebec were Vikings under the leadership of Leif Ericson. In A.D. 1000, Leif and thirty-five companions decided to investigate an old rumor of a land to the west. Unlike other Europeans of the time, the Vikings were not afraid to venture anywhere a ship would float. Their confidence was rewarded. The strange coastline was where it was said to be, and they explored it thoroughly from Newfoundland to Rhode Island. They could not possibly have missed the Kennebec.

They brought back glowing reports. Of chief interest was their description of great stands of pine. The Vikings always needed more timber for the building of the ships on which their economy depended. There were no forests at all in Iceland and Greenland, and Scandinavia, their homeland, was far away. So for about two centuries, voyages to Maine were commonplace and about as exciting to the Vikings as sending a truck to the lumberyard would be to us. Without doubt, the crews did a little hunting and fishing on these trips and explored the country to a small extent. But chiefly they tended to the business of cutting, loading, and transporting lumber.

Then even these visits stopped. The Abenakis at last began to resent the noisy strangers who chopped down their trees and frightened their game. They attacked landing parties successfully. Their weapons—powerful maple or ironwood bows, flint-tipped arrows, long spears, and heavy-headed tomahawks—were at least as good as those of the intruders. Moreover, the Indians had far greater numbers and were fighting on familiar ground. It became clear to the Norsemen that the wood they secured wasn't worth the danger involved; so they stopped coming. In another century or two the New World was completely forgotten.

Once in a while a bronze tool or weapon of Viking origin is found along the Maine coast. Aside from these small things, the Norse left no impression on the land or on its people. Trees grew back in the cuttings, landing places became overgrown with salt grass and sea lavender, the tides swept the shores clean of litter. The Abenakis didn't even pass on a legend of huge winged canoes sailing out of the rising sun. As far as Kennebec history is concerned, the Viking voyages might just as well have never taken place.

The real history of the white man along the river begins soon after the voyage of Columbus. His exploit laid at rest the principal fear of most European mariners that they would fall off the edge of a flat earth. Almost at once, ships of all nations set sail in search of a Northwest Passage to India. As early as 1497, John and Sebastian Cabot explored all the coast between Cape Cod and Newfoundland and claimed it for England. In 1524 and 1534, Cartier claimed the same territory for the French, thus sowing seeds of future bloodshed. These explorers were followed by others: Verrazano; the Spaniard Esteban Gomez, who gave Campobello its name; the Portugese Ferdinando; John Walker of England, who called the Kennebec country Norumbega; and many more. All were searching for a passage to India or for rich treasures of gold and jewels such as the Spaniards found in Mexico and Peru. All were doomed to disappointment.

Meanwhile, however, less ambitious voyages were being made

26

A Viking ship, c. A.D. *900 (the Viking Era).*

by countless nameless vessels manned by nameless captains and crews. These were the fishermen. By the mid-sixteenth century, the whole Maine coast was lively with businesslike little fleets. All the big, important explorers mentioned coming upon the small craft calmly loading up with cod, pollock, haddock, and hake for the fish-hungry Catholic countries of Europe.

A fishing smack usually made two voyages a year. As soon as it arrived on the Maine coast, a crew was put ashore to build drying stages where the catches could be cured for shipment home. Fresh fish would not keep on the long voyage. The men in charge of the drying lived ashore in rude cabins. Often they were left behind to guard company property when the ship sailed away.

While waiting for their ship's return, these men had plenty of time to become acquainted with the land and with the Indians. They did a little hunting, picked berries, established a friendly relationship with their native neighbors and traded for a few furs on the side. Many grew to love this strange, harsh land of rock and forest and put off from year to year returning home. Some of them never went back. They were the true first settlers along the lower Kennebec, although no one remembers their names.

The dream of fabulous stores of treasure in Norumbega died hard, but die at last it did. In its place grew a recognition of the true wealth of the great forested and sea-girt domain, the lumber, furs, and fish. The expeditions that set out between 1575 and 1605 were instructed not to waste time looking for diamond mines and Northwest Passages, but to bring back careful and detailed reports on Norumbega—its climate and weather, its natural resources, vegetation, soil, and water courses. Any knowledge that would throw light on the question of how to make the most of this new land was welcome.

Among this new breed of explorers were such practical men as George Weymouth, Bartholomew Gosnold, Martin Pring, and John Smith of Pocahontas fame. They brought back such encouraging reports of the possibilities of the region that companies were formed in England to promote trade and even settlement in Norumbega. Prominent men of the day were behind these companies: such men as Sir Walter Raleigh and his half brother Sir Humphrey Gilbert; Sir Ferdinando Gorges, who came to be known as the Father of Maine, although he never set foot on her soil; and Sir John Popham, the Lord Chief Justice of England. They themselves took no part in the actual exploration and development of the area. Their responsibility was to publicize the new land, to raise money for the outfitting of ships and hiring of crews, and to attend to such legal details as land grants and deeds of ownership. For their services, they received most of whatever money might be made.

In May, 1607, the Plymouth Company, which held grants to Norumbega, sent out the first group of colonists to North America. The largest stockholder in the company was Sir John Popham, and the expedition was led by his son George and Raleigh Gilbert, son of Sir Humphrey Gilbert. In the fall of that year the party of 120 men, recruited mostly from English jails, landed on the west shore of the Kennebec's mouth at what is now Popham.

They built a fort, houses, and storehouses. With them was Richard Seymour, an Episcopalian clergyman, so they built him a church as well. Petty criminals though they might be, the colonists knew how to work and how to use tools. Then, before snow fell, they explored the Kennebec through Merrymeeting Bay and up the Androscoggin as far as the present site of Brunswick. According to the journal that they faithfully kept, they

Sir John Popham.

found "the Countrey stored with Grapes white and red, good Hops, Onions, Garlick, Okes, Walnuts and soile good." They felt very optimistic about the future of their colony.

Autumn on the coast of Maine is unbelievably beautiful. The earth throbs with color—the flame of the maples, the shining copper of the tamaracs, the scarlet carpet of the blueberry bushes, the dark green of spruce and fir, all against the deep diamond-studded blue of the sea. The air is sparkling and clear as crystal and deceptively mild with Indian summer's belated glow. Kennebec farmers of today know better than to trust in this false summer; but the Popham colonists had had no experience with Maine weather. Accustomed to the comparatively mild English climate, they had no idea at all of how tough a Kennebec winter can be.

The winter of 1607–1608 was even worse than average. The new settlers recorded that "On the 18 Januarie we had in seven houres space thunder, lightning, raine, frost, snow, all in abundance, the last continuing." The houses were too thin-walled to keep out the bitter cold, and many of the colonists, including George Popham, died of pneumonia. The supplies that had been left them by their ships ran out. Townsmen that most of them were, they knew nothing about hunting and trapping for food. Scurvy developed among them. They heaped so much wood on the fires in order to keep somewhere near warm that they set fire to some of the buildings. It was a thoroughly miserable time.

So when the ships returned in the spring with more supplies, most of the sick, hungry, disheartened colonists wanted only to go home. They bundled aboard without regret and sailed off to leave to Jamestown the distinction of being the first permanent English settlement in America.

31

A few hardy souls remained behind. Perhaps they had come to love the country in spite of everything; or perhaps they decided that the new land, inhospitable as it might be, was better than a return to an English prison. Whatever became of this handful nobody knows. They were not at Popham when the next comers landed. They may have joined the Indians, or sailed out to Monhegan, which was more or less continuously inhabited by English fishermen at the time. Or they may have moved to Pemaquid, where there are unexplained foundations of very old buildings. Probably they survived somehow; they were a tough lot.

The Pophamites accomplished one thing before illness and the weather laid them low. They built a boat. This was the "pretty Pynnace" *Virginia of Sagadahoc* of thirty tons. She was the first ship to be built and launched by Europeans in the New World, the first of the long, long line that was to go out from the mouth of the Kennebec to the far corners of the globe. She was a good, sturdy little vessel and long outlasted the ill-fated colony. Her first voyage, that very spring of 1608, was to England with a cargo of Maine furs and sassafras root. Then for over twenty years she shuttled back and forth between England and Virginia, carrying supplies one way and tobacco the other. Finally she was wrecked in a storm off the Irish coast. She wasn't very big and she wasn't very fancy, but she set a standard of seaworthiness and dependability for all the great fleet of Kennebec-built ships to come.

After Popham collapsed, the English fishermen resumed their place as the first families of the Kennebec. By 1615 the whole adjacent coast was studded with fishing settlements. There is no way of knowing how many people were homesteading in Maine before the Pilgrim Fathers ever set foot on Plymouth Rock. The village on Monhegan Island had been well established for some

The Castle of Fort Pemaquid.

time, and from there settlers naturally drifted to the mainland. By 1623 there were flourishing little towns at Saco, Biddeford, Pemaquid, Bath, and along Merrymeeting Bay.

All this territory was ruled by Sir Ferdinando Gorges, who received a charter to the land between the Piscataqua and the Kennebec from the Plymouth Company. He was made the Governor General of New England, as the area had become known. This office carried with it the absolute powers of a king. The charter specified that the grant should "forever be called the Province and Countie of Maine and not by any other name whatsoever." Thus was Maine named, but to this day no one is sure where the name came from.

Gorges never visited Maine, so the settlers lived in complete freedom from authority. The same story was repeated over and over: a clearing in the pines, corn planted, vegetables raised and stored in earth cellars such as the Indians used, fish dried on stages, women spinning, men digging out stumps, small families growing and sending their sons to new clearings. Then at a convenient central location, some enterprising soul would open a store. Soon a tavern, a gristmill and a little church were added—and a new town was born. Gradually all the coast west of the Penobscot blossomed with these English hamlets.

In the meantime, almost identical villages were springing up to the east, along the St. Croix River. The French had not been idle in their share of the New World. In 1604 they had built a colony on Dochet Island, in the St. Croix opposite what is now Calais, Maine. This colony, unlike Popham, was successful, and from it French explorers and settlers branched out. In these far Down East villages French was spoken instead of English, worship was held in Catholic chapels instead of Protestant churches, and

34

pot au feu was cooked instead of deer-meat stew. Otherwise the lives of the people were just the same.

Later, as they expanded, the two nationalities were to come into conflict; but in the early days each group was too busy getting a foothold in the wilderness to bother the other. All anybody wanted was to be let alone to tend his own affairs. So for a while all was peaceful along the Kennebec; or at least as peaceful as any place can be where people, with their human differences, live side by side.

U. S. 1382873

Four CUSHNOC

Just as many of the Kennebec's present-day towns grew out of fishing villages, others began as fur trading posts. Fur was as valuable as fish, and like fishing, fur trading was older than any settlement. In 1615, Sir John Hawkins picked up a cargo of pelts on one of his trips along the coast and sold it in Europe at a handsome profit. This deal, along with a sudden passion among the fashionable for beaver hats, caused the fur trade to boom. But it had already been going on for a long time. Way back in the days of the first explorers, any ship touching the coast exchanged the skins that the Indians brought down to landing places for knives, beads, bright kerchiefs, or any other cheap gewgaws that caught the savages' fancy. The business was profitable, but until 1628 it was carried on in a rather haphazard manner.

In that year, the Pilgrim Fathers of Plymouth found themselves in need of money. They had rented the *Mayflower* on a go-now-pay-later plan, and the payments were coming due. Their eight-year-old colony was self-supporting, but they had no hard cash and no way of raising any. Corn, beans, and squash were all right for barter among themselves and with the Indians, but certainly would not satisfy their creditors in England. They looked around for possibilities and decided that their best bet was to go into the fur trade.

The fur-bearing animals of eastern Massachusetts were few and not very valuable. Maine, which was a part of Massachusetts at the time, seemed to the Pilgrims to be the best place for their enterprise. They chose three spots for their trading posts. Two did not last long. The one at Machias was soon destroyed by the French, who did not relish competition so near their borders. The second at Pentagoet, now Castine, continued for a few years until the French put it, too, out of business. The third prospered long after the *Mayflower* debt had been paid in full.

This one was located about forty miles up the Kennebec at a place called Cushnoc, now Augusta and the state capital. Cushnoc means "the tide runs no further up the river." The Abenakis attached special meaning to this fact and had always used the tide-head at Cushnoc as a meeting place for political and religious pow-wows. Cushnoc was ideal for Pilgrim purposes. It was at a safe distance from the French, the small ships of the day could easily sail that far up the river, and the Indians were already in the habit of gathering there.

The post at Cushnoc lasted for almost forty years, during which no trouble at all occurred with either the French or the Abenakis. The only trouble to arise was between the Plymouth traders and another Englishman. It resulted in the first murder to be recorded in Maine.

This is what happened. Soon after the post was established, an independent trapper named Hocking started running his own trap lines and doing his own bargaining with the Indians. The Pilgrims, for all their piety, were hard-headed operators. They did not like the idea of an outsider cutting in on their territory. The Cushnoc factor, John Howland, told Hocking to move on. Hocking told Howland to try and make him. It was a free country and he had as much right there as anyone. This is the way that Kennebec men, down to the present day, are apt to respond when someone tries to push them around.

In the fight that followed this exchange of hot words, Hocking was shot in the head. Everybody at the post agreed that he had got exactly what he had asked for and that it served him right. The body was buried and the matter was dismissed.

This, however, was not the end. There happened to be a trade ship anchored in the river at the time, captained by John Alden of Plymouth—the shy hero of Longfellow's *The Courtship of Miles Standish*. When he arrived back in Boston with his load of furs, Alden mentioned the shooting of Hocking simply as a mildly interesting piece of Kennebec Valley gossip. He had had nothing to do with the killing. He had not even seen it happen. Nevertheless, he was immediately arrested and thrown into jail as a suspect.

Plymouth had always been jealous of Boston, and the Pilgrim leaders were furious at this insult to one of their own. They sent Miles Standish to Boston to get Alden out of his difficulties. Standish was not a patient man and during his years of soldiering he had picked up a vocabulary that was far from gentlemanly. He unwisely used this on Governor Dudley of Boston, who was hearing Alden's case. Dudley was so enraged by Standish's violent language that he turned John Alden loose and arrested Standish instead. Standish was jailed on the same charges that had been held against Alden. This was pretty silly, since Standish was three hundred miles from Cushnoc when Hocking was killed.

But from there on, everybody forgot about poor Hocking. Boston and Plymouth were too busy dragging up old grudges to bother about finding the murderer of an unimportant fur trapper way back in the wilds. Finally the whole business was dropped. John Alden married Standish's girl, Hocking's killer went unpunished, and the Pilgrims had no more trouble with poachers at Cushnoc.

38

Maine's Capitol at Augusta. G. Henri Desmond, architect.

The seeds of a far more serious trouble lay at Cushnoc, however. This had nothing to do with furs, trapping privileges, French and English claims to the territory, or private murders. It was something quite different. We have said that a river may be a highway. The great highway of the Kennebec reached into the heart of Maine and almost to the Canadian border. This made it easy for the Canadian Indians, who were more or less under French rule, to bring their canoe-loads of pelts down to Cushnoc to trade.

The French knew this, but they were not much concerned about it. They already had all the furs they could handle, thanks to Samuel de Champlain. Champlain had been an explorer, probably America's greatest, and he knew the country and the natives well. At his suggestion, years before, the French had begun to send young Frenchmen to live among the Indians as tribe members. These young men were called *coureurs de bois*, or woods runners, forest rangers. They did not try to civilize the Indians, but only to understand them and win their friendship. They were a wild, brave, restless lot, more at home in the wilderness than in towns. Some of them became almost more Indian than the Indians themselves. They passed freely and unharmed through the forest as far west as the Great Lakes. Because the Indians liked and trusted them, they were able to secure fortunes in fabulous furs for the French. The few pelts that trickled down the Kennebec to Cushnoc didn't seem worth worrying about.

After a while, however, the Jesuit missionaries in Canada began to hear disturbing rumors. The Indians who had been to Cushnoc reported that their friends along the Kennebec were being converted to the Protestant faith by the English traders and their ministers. This was something that the devout Catholic Fathers could not ignore. Their purpose in coming to the New World was to save the souls of the heathen. Something, plainly, would have to be done about the souls being led astray at Cushnoc.

Five

In 1649, Father Gabriel Druillettes set out from Quebec to undo the damage done by the Protestants of Cushnoc. He was accompanied by Indian guides. The party went up the Chaudière River, no mean feat in itself. Chaudière means boiling, and that is exactly what the river looks like—a kettle of madly boiling water. Then they crossed the height of land and came out on the banks of the Kennebec. This was easy enough for the Abenakis in their practical buckskins; but for Father Druillettes in the flowing black robes of the Church, there must have been difficult times.

There must have been satisfactions as well. Father Druillettes was the first white man ever to follow the course of the upper Kennebec. It is always thrilling to be a pioneer, to be *first*. He was the first white ever to set eyes on the awesome bulk of Katahdin, the Indian's sacred mountain. That alone must have made worthwhile the long, grueling journey. Years later, Benedict Arnold on his disastrous march to Quebec led his homespun army over the trail blazed by Druillettes. Today Maine State Highway 201, used every summer by thousands of tourists in their comfortable cars, follows the same route.

Father Druillettes established a mission at Norridgewock, about fifty miles upriver from Cushnoc. Here he worked to convert the Abenakis to his faith. Like most of the Jesuit missionaries, he was selfless, devout, capable, and understanding. So his mission was extremely successful. What is more surprising, he got along well with the traders down at Cushnoc; surprising, because Catholicism was considered terrible beyond words by the English Protestants. But once, when Father Druillettes visited Massachusetts, he was entertained in the home of John Winslow, a Cushnoc factor from Plymouth.

Father Druillettes' place was taken in time by Father Sebastien Râle. The Abenakis had loved Druillettes. They practically idolized Râle. He worried about their standard of living, their education, and their general welfare as well as about their religion. He lived among them as one of themselves, going hungry when they went hungry, sharing their bad fortune and their good. When he thought they were being cheated or mistreated by the white men, and they often were, he came to their defense. Nobody else had bothered to record Indian customs and laws. He did. He worked continually on a book about such matters. He spoke Abenaki well and compiled a dictionary of the language. He trained a choir of forty Indians to sing church music in their own tongue. Today the descendants of the Norridgewock converts still use some of the prayers that Father Râle translated into Abenaki. His native parishioners adored him, and for a while he got along with the English fairly well.

But trouble between the French and the English was brewing elsewhere. They were beginning to overlap on each other's claims to territory. The English had by now cultivated much of the Kennebec Valley from the sea to Cushnoc and beyond, turning the area into an almost continuous farm. The French, who contended that all the land as far south as the Kennebec belonged to them, had set up trading posts at various points along the coast. Off and on, groups of one nation came into conflict with groups of the other. These were purely local squabbles and of little interest to those not actually involved in the fighting. In time, however,

43

Mount Katáhdin.

this simmering pot was to boil over into the French and Indian Wars.

An important French trading post was at Pentagoet on the Penobscot, the same post that the French had taken away from the Pilgrims years before. This was almost the private property of a man with the very fancy name of Jean Vincent de l'Abadie, Baron de Castin.

Castin, as he is usually known, had an unusual history. He was a nobleman whose family owned huge estates in France, and he was what would probably be considered a juvenile delinquent now-a-days. Not that he was really bad. He was just wild, with too much money and too much family influence for his own good. He caused his parents so much trouble that they saw to it, when he was fifteen, that he enlist in the French army and arranged to have him sent to Quebec on overseas duty. This was supposed to be a punishment that would discipline Castin into being a better and more obedient boy.

It didn't work out that way. From the moment he set foot in the New World, he felt completely at home for the first time in his life. Instead of staying in the barracks and polishing his boots and buttons, as he was supposed to do, he took every opportunity to slip away to the Indian villages. He and the Indians became bosom companions. When his enlistment expired, he refused to go home. Instead, he legally married in the Catholic Church the daughter of a powerful Abenaki chief and was adopted into the tribe. Then he went into the fur-trading business at Pentagoet. Because of his useful connection with the Indians, he made a fortune in furs.

When the ill-feeling between the French and the English developed into actual war, Castin was on one of his long trips into the wilderness. He had no way of keeping in touch with current events. He first learned of the state of affairs when he returned to Pentagoet to find that the English had raided the place. They had taken away all his bales of furs and anything else of value. Worse, they had left a message that Castin could have his property back if he had the nerve to go to Pemaquid after it.

One quality Castin did not lack was nerve, and another was temper. This insult drove him almost mad with rage. He immediately declared a personal war on the English, a war that lasted twenty years. First, with a quickly assembled band of devoted Abenakis, he went to Pemaquid and completely destroyed the village. Before he was done, he had burned countless towns, including Falmouth—now Portland—to the ground. His name came to be feared more than that of the Devil. English mothers along the Kennebec and the coast used it to terrify children into being good.

But before all this happened, the Kennebec English rather tardily realized that Father Râle had a dangerously strong hold on Abenaki loyalty. They induced a Protestant minister, the Reverend Joseph Baxter, to come to Brunswick to reconvert the Indians. They even offered to throw in a schoolteacher to teach Abenaki children to read and write, if Abenaki parents would turn to Protestantism. The Indians were not impressed. They let Mr. Baxter build a church, but they refused to attend it.

The year 1721 saw an outbreak of violence after a term of uneasy peace. The Indians killed cows and other livestock along the Kennebec and threatened to do worse things. The English government replied by demanding that the Abenakis surrender Father Râle, whom they now considered Public Enemy Number Two, after Castin. When that demand had no effect, they placed a price of five hundred pounds on the missionary's head.

In an attempt to collect this bounty, a Captain Westbrook marched a troup to Norridgewock through the snow of a Kennebec winter. He found the nest, but the bird had flown. He burned the chapel and destroyed all the manuscripts on which Râle had worked hard for so long. But Râle was tough and stubborn. Almost before the ashes of Norridgewock were cold, he and his Abenakis started to rebuild.

But the little French mission was doomed. In August of 1724, seventeen whaleboats carrying two hundred armed English soldiers and several Mohawk guides moved quietly up the river. No one was on guard, since no guard had been needed for three years. Some of the Indians were fishing on the river, others were busy with camp chores or simply loafing around, and Father Râle was lying down after an active day. Suddenly death struck with a roar of musketry and a rain of bullets. Almost no one escaped.

Father Râle was shot by a half-breed named Jacques, who was in the pay of the English. Jaquish Island, a desolate place of bare rock and bitter surf, keeps alive the name of the man who killed the best friend the Kennebec Abenakis ever had.

With Râle's death, the entire Kennebec was at last open to the English. It was an expensive victory, though. The grief and anger of the Abenakis knew no bounds, and they fought like fiends to avenge Râle. He had lived so that his name, when remembered, would stand for service, brotherhood, and love of his fellow man. It seems strange that in the end it was used as a rallying cry to death and destruction along the river where he had spent more than half his years.

Six THE TIME OF TERROR

The story of the Kennebec Valley between 1675 and 1763 is a story of homes standing in flame and feet running desperately in the night; of bloodcurdling screams in the darkness and women and little children walking through the wilderness in the dead of winter to Quebec. It is the chilling tale of people who from childhood to old age never slept soundly and easily. Always they went to bed with the terrible knowledge that dawn might well find everything for which they had worked so hard reduced to ashes and they themselves either dead or in captivity. Such were the French and Indian Wars.

Actually there were six of these wars—King Philip's, King William's, Queen Ann's, Lovewell's and King George's Wars, and the Sixth War. It is easier, though, to think of them as one long war, interrupted occasionally by periods of brittle truce.

The underlying cause of the war lay in Europe, where France and England were struggling for supremacy. It might have remained a war between the French and the English, with the Indians about equally divided in their sympathies, if the English settlers had shown any imagination at all in their treatment of the redmen. But from earliest days, they had been indifferent to the feelings of the natives, while the French had been considerate and understanding. When the active fighting started, the Indians had no trouble in choosing sides.

The war began in Massachusetts, when a Wampanoag chief known as King Philip rebelled against the continued abuse and cheating of his people by the English. It quickly spread north and east to Maine, where the Abenakis were already discontented and sullen over the way they were being treated. In almost no time, the valley of the Kennebec was a shambles. Woolwich, Arrowsic, Pemaquid, Damariscotta, and a dozen other flourishing little villages were completely destroyed. The settlers who survived and escaped captivity fled to the offshore islands, there to wait out the hostilities. Some of them never returned, but started anew in these safer places.

Gradually the colonists learned. They learned that it was hopeless for each family to try to protect its own single home against Indian attack. Therefore in each area one central house with a good water supply was chosen for a stronghold. It was surrounded by a high stockade, the upper story was rebuilt to overhang the lower, the walls were pierced with loopholes, and the roof was covered with sod to prevent fire from the flame-tipped arrows of the raiders. At the first hint of trouble, everyone living nearby hurried to this fortification, bringing with them as much food and as many valuables as they could carry. The cattle were driven inside the stockade, and the great gate was closed and barred. Then it was a matter of waiting in dread for whatever was to come.

Often there was not time for people living on the outskirts to reach the stockade. Then they had to defend themselves as best they were able. The success of most Indian raids depended on surprise. The savages were masters of the art of making themselves inconspicuous. They could drift through the forest like shadows, live off the country, go for long periods without fire with its betraying smoke, and crouch as still and patient as stones hour after hour. Often a whole war party would lie within shouting distance of a homestead for days, and not even the dogs were the wiser. When the time was ripe, they swooped down on their objective. They were terrible in their war paint, and their unearthly whooping chilled the blood. Sometimes individuals escaped by hiding in cornfields, cellars, or even under beds and in ovens, but not often.

Both the French and the English paid the Indians a bounty for scalps. The French, in addition, paid handsome sums for captives. That is why so many were taken. The men would have caused too much trouble on the long journey north. They were usually killed on the spot and scalped for the bounty. Women and children were more easily managed, and the raiders showed them a certain amount of rough consideration. It was to their best interests. The more healthy captives delivered, the greater the reward.

Once in Canada, the captives were handed over to the French. Some of them were placed in French homes as servants, some of the girls were entered in convents, and surprisingly often small children were adopted into French families. They were treated well. Moreover, there was always the chance and hope that the captives would be ransomed and could go home. When this happened, most of them were happy to return to their own people.

Once in a while it didn't work out that way. One Kennebec girl, carried away to Montreal when she was ten, at seventeen married a prosperous Frenchman. A few years later, she was rescued by her brother and returned to the valley in which she had spent her childhood. Her blood relatives were strangers to her. Everything about their lives—the hard farm work, the simple food, the plain clothing, the lack of entertainment—seemed harsh and outlandish to her after the busy, colorful life of the French city. She was homesick for her French family and friends, for the easy French laughter and the quick French speech. After a short visit, she packed her clothes and went back to Canada. Her English family was not sorry to see her go. She and her Frenchified ways made them uncomfortable.

Wars always throw certain figures into the limelight. William Phips, however, didn't need the French and Indian Wars to focus attention on him. As early as he knew anything, he knew that the life of a salt-water farmer on the lower Kennebec was not what he wanted. His twenty-one older brothers and four older sisters might be contented with things around Woolwich, where they were all born; but not he. As soon as he was old enough, he paddled a canoe across the river to Arrowsic and apprenticed himself to a shipwright. During the next four years, he heard hundreds of sailors tell their tall tales of high adventure in foreign lands. Naturally, he became filled with longing to join this glamorous brotherhood.

At the end of his apprenticeship, Phips worked his way to Boston and got a job as a ship carpenter. Boston was a revelation to him. Woolwich and Arrowsic were never like this! Being extremely intelligent as well as very ambitious, he saw immediately that his ignorance was a handicap. He taught himself to read and write—not just passably, but better than many educated men of the time. He then announced to anyone who would listen that he was going to captain one of the King's ships before he was through, and build a big brick house in Boston's best neighborhood. No one paid much attention.

Next, he somehow managed to meet and marry the beautiful daughter of Captain Roger Spencer. This must have been difficult for an unknown carpenter, but Phips was both handsome and full of self-confidence. He apparently swept the young lady off her feet. The marriage gave him important seafaring connections

51

A King's ship of the mid-1600's.

which he used to secure a contract to build a ship. Returning to the Kennebec, where labor and material were cheap, he set up a shipyard near his birthplace. At almost the exact moment when he was about to get his first vessel under way for delivery, Indians attacked the area. Phips piled the terrified settlers, including his mother, brothers, and sisters, aboard the ship and sailed them safely to Boston. This gave him a hero's reputation and led to the captaincy of a vessel in the West Indies trade. He'd had no training whatsoever as a mariner, but that didn't disturb him a bit. He was a fast learner.

In the West Indies, he heard about sunken treasure and decided that locating it was a quicker and more interesting path to fame and fortune than tamely sailing cargoes of lumber and molasses up and down the Atlantic could ever be. He went to England and somehow talked Charles II into letting him have the King's ship *Rose* of eighteen guns and a crew of ninety-five to use for the recovery of Spanish gold.

Looking for lost treasure is a chancy business at best; but the Phips luck held. He returned to England with over two million dollars' worth of gold, silver, and gems in the ship's hold. He was given his share, plus a gold chain and medal for himself, a gold cup worth five thousand dollars for his wife, and a knighthood. He arrived back in Boston as Sir William Phips, High Sheriff of Massachusetts. He at once built the brick house.

In 1690, the Massachusetts authorities became worried about the way things were going Down East. Trade was being ruined by the unsettled conditions. They suspected that Port Royal in Nova Scotia was outfitting and paying Indians to harass the Maine coast. Someone, clearly, had to deal with Port Royal; and who was better qualified than Sir William Phips? He set sail with a small fleet in

March of that year, and three months later he was back. He had captured and subdued not only Port Royal, but all of Nova Scotia as well. As a reward, Phips was made Royal Governor of Massachusetts, which of course included Maine.

Phips was a very good governor. Until his death in 1695, there was little trouble with the Indians, many of whom had played with William in childhood and knew and trusted him. He was buried in London, a far cry from the log cabin by the Kennebec where he was born. He was the first of the sons of the valley to achieve international renown.

The French, meanwhile, were strengthening their position in the New World. By the 1740's, they had built at Louisbourg the strongest fortress in the entire Western Hemisphere. It commanded the only good entrance into Canada, controlled the valuable offshore fisheries, and served as a base for a large fleet of privateers that continually hijacked English ships carrying valuable cargo. Finally the Maine coast fishermen and traders got tired of being preyed upon and suggested to the Massachusetts government that something be done about it. Their idea was that a force should be sent to capture Louisbourg and put an end to the annoyance.

This was obviously impossible. Louisbourg was the Gibraltar of America. It was very heavily fortified and garrisoned by a large force of trained soldiers. Moreover, the French were not likely to give up easily an installation into which they had poured over thirty million livres. Louis Vaughn of Damariscotta, near the mouth of the Kennebec, refused to recognize the impossible. He bedeviled the Massachusetts Assembly constantly. The difficulties were pointed out to him by more reasonable men. It would take a large fleet of battleships, a large army of disciplined soldiers, and a large amount of heavy artillery to even make a dent in Louisbourg. Massachusetts had none of these things, and England had made it clear that the colonists could expect no help from her in any such harebrained project. Vaughn had better go home and forget the whole matter.

But Vaughn made such a nuisance of himself that he finally wore the Assembly down into agreeing by one vote to the proposition. He secured that small margin only because an assemblyman fell down and broke his leg in his hurry to get to the meeting and vote against the idea. In March, 1745, the expedition set forth. It was ridiculous. The navy consisted of about ninety small fishing boats, most of them unarmed. The army was made up of fishermen, storekeepers, farmers, trappers and lumberjacks. It was commanded by William Pepperell, a merchant. All that could be said for it was that each man owned his own rifle and knew how to use it. As for artillery—there wasn't any. They decided to worry about cannon when they got to where they were going. Over half the adult male population of the Kennebec Valley was included in this sorry crowd.

The makeshift force had better luck than it deserved or could possibly have expected. Almost at once it fell in with a British squadron patrolling American waters that acted against orders and joined them. The coast of Nova Scotia at this time of year is usually battered by a tremendous icy surf and shrouded in dense fog. That year the sea was as calm as a mill pond and the air as clear as crystal. The army had no difficulty in landing and setting up camp by the wide marsh that protected the rear of Louisbourg. On the very first night, a scouting party managed, by using the skills they had learned in Indian fighting, to steal close and burn down the warehouses containing most of the food supply of the fortress. This dealt the French a bad blow at the very start. On their way back to camp, the scouts captured thirty cannon, worth their weight in gold to the besiegers.

The problem now was to move the cannon across the marsh to within firing range of the walls of Louisbourg. Sledges were built of logs, and horses and oxen were commandeered from the surrounding countryside to drag them. The animals proved useless. They panicked when they began to sink in the deep mire of the swamp. They were cut loose and men took their places in harness, two hundred men to a sledge.

Soon the mud was churned into hip-deep soup into which the guns were in danger of sinking out of sight. Causeways had to be built under the fire of the fortress' artillery. It was a terrible and heartbreaking task, performed by men whose shoes were rotting off their feet, whose clothes had been worn to tatters, and whose bodies were racked with chills and fevers brought on by being always wet in the raw cold of a Cape Breton spring. Hundreds of them died beside the dreadful marsh, and more were to live with rheumatic pain for the rest of their lives. But still the survivors advanced.

Two months after the ridiculous expedition from the New England coast first landed, the Gibraltar of America surrendered to it. The gaunt veterans of the ordeal of the swamp were now free to return to the farms and fish piers that were home.

Three short years later, in 1748, the Treaty of Aix-la-Chapelle was signed. By its terms, the English gave Louisbourg back to the French. Anger flamed all along the Maine coast and up the Kennebec. Men who rose each morning with aching joints and went about their day's work handicapped by ruined health were filled with bitterness. They felt that they had suffered for nothing and that their heroic efforts were being belittled. They began to wonder bleakly just exactly how interested the Crown was in the welfare of its overseas subjects. Perhaps the colonies would be better off without . . .

Nobody yet finished the traitorous thought, even privately. But the seed of discontent with British rule had been planted. Even after Wolfe captured Quebec in 1759 and all Canada came under English rule, it lay there. It would take time to sprout and grow; but time was like the river. It flowed along, slowly, perhaps, but surely.

Seven

During the Revolution that had been brewing for so long, only one military campaign of any importance was conducted on Maine soil. The little province made her contribution, of course. Over six thousand men—a very large percent of the small population—fought on land and sea. There were Kennebec Valley men at Ticonderoga, Monmouth, Stillwater, and Saratoga. Almost one tenth of Washington's force at Valley Forge hailed from Maine. But the fighting took place on other battlefields.

In 1775, General Washington decided to carry the war into Canadian territory. He ordered Colonel Benedict Arnold to march on Quebec and capture the city. The route was to be through Maine for two reasons. It was the shortest way by land; and surprise was more likely if the army approached through uninhabited wilderness than if it came openly by sea.

Arnold was given about eleven hundred men from southern New England, Pennsylvania, and Virginia. These were all experienced veterans of Indian fighting, tough and wily, expert in the use of the long rifle, the tomahawk, and the scalping knife. They were completely at home in the woods, too—or at least, the woods of their native areas. They did not yet know that the Maine woods are something else again. The trail chosen was that of old Father Druillettes in reverse: up the Kennebec, across the height of land to the Chaudière, and so to Quebec.

Eleven schooners took Arnold's force from Newburyport, N.H., to Pittston, a few miles below the old trading post of

Cushnoc on the Kennebec. Here a Major Colburn was building two hundred bateaux on order for the expedition. They were joined by a company of Maine men under the command of Samuel McCobb of Georgetown, a village at the mouth of the river. These men had not been ordered to come. But they had all fought at Bunker Hill during the preceding June, and now in September they decided that it was time for them to take another crack at the British. The rest of Arnold's army looked on the whole thing as a glorious adventure. Only McCobb's little band, Maine born and raised, recognized the difficulties ahead.

The campaign began with a three-day barbecue at Fort Western, as Cushnoc was now known. This was a very gay affair. Three bears were roasted whole, and there was plenty of venison, beef, pork, and wild fowl as well. The settlers of the neighborhood contributed green corn, squash, melons, and potatoes, and their wives baked hundreds of pies and loaves of bread. Everyone for miles around attended. There were frequent toasts and a great deal of singing. It was fun, even though it wasn't very military.

Finally the fun was over, and the serious business of getting to Quebec began. Immediately it became clear that the bateaux were third-rate. Major Colburn had not had enough seasoned lumber on hand for so many boats, and he had had to use green pine and oak. What's more, he had built hastily and with little care, knowing that the plan called for the craft to be abandoned at the Chaudière. They were, therefore, much too heavy and handled badly. Moreover, as the timber dried, they leaked like sieves and went to pieces at the slightest strain. By the time the fifty miles to Norridgewock had been covered, much of the glamour had rubbed off the adventure.

At Norridgewock, worse trouble developed. The expedition

had set out with a hundred tons of provisions. Now it was found that the beef, cured in hot weather, was rotten, and that constant soaking in the leaky bateaux had caused the peas, beans, and hard-tack to mold. Everything had to be thrown away except the salt pork and the flour. Before it was even well started, the expedition found itself on half rations. There were still a few backwoods farms where cattle could be bought for slaughter, and game was occasionally killed for meat. But bargaining and hunting took time.

And time was precious. The planners of the campaign had not realized how early winter comes to Maine, nor how severe it can be. By October first there was windowpane ice in the swamps; ice thick enough to bar the passage of a boat, but not thick enough to bear the weight of a man; ice that cut through clothes and leather boots like a knife. The Virginians and the Pennsylvanians, accustomed to the bland and lovely autumns of the South, were miserable in the iron cold. Pneumonia and dysentery developed among them. Those who could still walk were sent back, and the others left in a crude log hospital to wait for recovery or death.

The rest struggled on. They cut their way through dense tangles of blow-down, floundered through swamps, toiled almost inch by inch up the height of land. More and more equipment was abandoned—spoiled food, heavy cooking utensils, chests of ammunition, even guns and axes. Over a century later, bateaux were found here, preserved in the mire of the bogs, where exhausted men had dropped them. Game was very scarce now, so the dogs that many of the men had brought with them were killed and eaten. It turned suddenly warm, and drenching rains fell. Streams rose four or five feet in a single night. A third of the army gave up and turned back, taking more than their fair share of the provisions with them. There were now less than five hundred left of the light-hearted throng that had sung and feasted at Fort Western.

The scouts who had been sent ahead to find a way to the Chaudière returned. They were walking skeletons, but they had done their work. They had blazed a trail to the river. On the tired remnant of an army labored. Their clothes were in rags now, and their boots long gone. The leather tops had been boiled to make soup in which there might be some slight nourishment. The men's feet were bound in rags, as long as the rags lasted. But the scouts had brought back word that the French inhabitants across the Chaudière were eager to help the Americans. This hope spurred them on.

The Chaudière was a cauldron, like its name. The last bateau was smashed into kindling, and most of the guns were lost. All the food was gone now. The men ate their leather cartridge boxes and dug in the sand for roots. Many left their bones by the boiling river. Only stubbornness and the last shreds of hope kept the others going.

Then at last the river was crossed and the terrible trek through the wilderness was over. Ahead lay the pleasant fields and comfortable farmhouses of the *habitants*. These French country people were amazed at the appearance of the men who had come through such an ordeal. The rumor spread that the Americans were dressed in armor. Their skin had been weathered to the color of iron and was almost as hard.

The sympathetic French provided the scarecrow horde with food, shelter, and care. Enough moccasins were found to replace the vanished boots. Clothes were mended and illnesses treated. For the first time in two months the exhausted and starving Americans knew what it was to sleep in deep, comfortable featherbeds and to eat well-prepared, well-seasoned meals. Their strength returned quickly, and the rested army was reorganized for the march to the St. Lawrence.

When they arrived there, they found to their dismay that all boats had been taken to the other side of the river, and that two British men-of-war were on patrol. But Arnold spirited his men across on rafts in the dead of night, right under the noses of the patrol. They landed at Wolfe's Cove and climbed his path to the Plains of Abraham. Then the wind came up and the moon burst from the clouds. At last the invaders could see the great citadel that they had come to capture. The little band of three hundred and fifty men looked pretty insignificant on the wide plain beneath the towering walls.

At daybreak the Quebec soldiers and citizens came out on the rampart and cheered the Americans. This was not ridicule, but a genuine tribute to the foolhardy courage that had brought them through the hell of the winter wilderness. The ragamuffin band offered no threat to the city, so the population could afford to be generous. Even Arnold had to admit that the situation was hopeless. He reluctantly retreated twenty miles and sat down to wait for Montgomery, who was supposed to reinforce him by sea.

Montgomery arrived on the first of December. Still the invading force waited for a blizzard to cover its attack. A month later it came, and Arnold and Montgomery advanced on opposite sides of the city. Almost at once Arnold received a cannon ball in the knee and had to be carried to the rear on his men's shoulders. Montgomery was killed outright. The leaderless men were trapped under the barricades, and two hundred of them were shot down from the high, overlooking windows. A few escaped over the ice of the river and the rest were captured. Many of them died later on, while in prison, of scurvey and smallpox.

Maine's only Revolutionary campaign was over. Arnold's army was demolished and nothing remained of the high hopes with which it had left Fort Western. The agony in the forest was for nothing. All that came out of the ill-fated expedition was a legend of courage and endurance that still lives in the valley of the Kennebec. Perhaps it is enough.

Eight

After the Revolution ended with American independence, the people along the Kennebec were free at last to develop their valley without interference. The Indians were no longer a menace. Attacks from the French and the British were a thing of the past. Now a man could settle down to the business of making a living and a place for himself in the world. Massachusetts offered any would-be settler one hundred and fifty acres on a river at a dollar an acre, or a hundred acres free away from a watercourse. People flocked to Maine. Along with this rise in population, industry boomed.

Since the little Popham *Virginia of Sagadahoc,* shipbuilding had always been an important part of the Kennebec scene. On a larger or smaller scale, about everybody in the valley was a shipbuilder. Each little salt-water or riverbank farm had, down on the shore, its own small shipways. Here, between planting and haying and haying and harvest, the men and boys of the family worked on the family sloop or ketch. A boat was as necessary to them as a pick-up truck is to the farmer of today.

The boys who learned to caulk a seam at the age of six grew up to be skilled shipwrights. They found employment in the big commercial shipyards of Brunswick and especially Bath. Ever since William Swanton had launched the first full-rigged ship there, the waterfront of Bath had rung with the sound of hammer and saw. It was the perfect place for building and launching ships. The banks of the Long Reach sloped at just the right angle, and the channel ran in close and deep to the shore. More ships were built on the Long Reach than on any other three-mile stretch in the world. Finally, English shipwrights appealed to the King to limit Bath shipbuilding. The competition was ruining them.

Another source of discontent between the colonies and the Crown was the mast pines. For years before the Revolution, the Royal Navy had suffered from a shortage of masts. This was bad enough to endanger national safety. There were plenty of the best masts on earth in Maine—the giant white pines that soared two hundred flawless feet into the air. But the settlers were cutting them down right and left, to split into clapboards, floorboards and shingles, or simply to clear the land for planting.

So in 1691, the King made a new rule for the colonists. From then on, all white pine measuring more than twenty-four inches at a foot from the ground belonged to the Crown. To make sure that there was no misunderstanding, mast agents of the King marked all such trees with three ax slashes in the shape of a broad arrow. This brand identified all property of the British Admiralty. Anyone cutting one of these marked pines was fined one hundred pounds. The resourceful Kennebec settlers made almost a game of thinking up ways to use the trees without getting caught. Many old Kennebec houses still standing today have floorboards of the beautiful honey-colored wood, trimmed down to just under the illegal twenty-four inches.

After the Revolution, the King no longer had a say in Maine affairs. Now there was a different problem. Before the Revolution, Kennebec ships engaged in the three-cornered slave-molasses-and-rum trade between Africa, the West Indies and the home ports, and the equally profitable transportation of fish, lumber, cotton, tobacco, farm produce, and furs to Europe. At the end of the war,

65

this commerce had been wiped out. A great many ships had been sunk or captured by the British, and a new merchant marine would have to be built. This was not too serious. The Maine shipyards could easily restore the fleet, given a little time.

The real problem was where to send the new ships. By English law, no foreign vessels—and American vessels were now foreign—were allowed to trade with England or any of her many possessions. This cut off the rum and slave trade, and a large part of all other commerce as well. The only place left was the Orient, where trade had always been completely in the hands of the British East India Company. No one had ever dared to dispute its monopoly.

In 1784, however, Captain John Greene defied tradition by sailing his *Empress of China* from New York to Canton. This was the first voyage ever made directly to China. Greene came home with a rich cargo of tea, silks, porcelain, and spices. He made such a tremendous profit that all shipowners, including those of the Kennebec, at once decided to follow his example.

This was the beginning of the fabulous era of the China Trade. During this glamorous period the famous clipper ships were developed. Speed was important. Some cargoes suffered if they were kept too long at sea. The first ship in from China was able to command the top prices for its merchandise and skimmed the cream off the market. So ship designers bent over their drawing boards, pondering ways to make sailing vessels faster. Little by little, the clippers were evolved. They were slim and sleek-lined, traveling like the wind under their towering clouds of canvas. They have been called the most beautiful objects ever made by American craftsmen. They were sailed by men with nerves of steel. The captains of the rather tubby ships of the East India Company were aghast at the daring of the Yankee seamen, who piled on sail until

67

A frigate.

masts bent like bows, and who refused to lay-to in the worst of weather.

Down the Atlantic the clippers raced with their cargoes of beef, salt cod, pickled salmon, barrel staves, lumber, and sugar. Then they faced the rounding of Cape Horn, the place in the world most dreaded by sailors for its terrible storms, paralyzing cold, dense fogs, and deadly icebergs. The bones of many a Kennebec boy lie on the ocean floor off the Horn. That peril behind them, the clippers drove across the Pacific toward Asia, where Malayan pirates lurked and purple coral-heads lay beneath the blue waters to tear the bottom out of a ship. The China trade did not offer a safe and easy life.

But the rewards were great. During this period the gracious houses that can be seen today in Bath and Brunswick, Wiscasset and other Kennebec towns were built. They were filled with beautiful furniture, fabrics, and objects of art from far corners of the globe. They belonged to the owners and captains of the clippers, the lovely ships with the lovely names.

Not all the benefits could be seen and touched. Very often captains took their families along with them on the long voyages. Little boys learned mathematics by helping their fathers plot a ship's position, and little girls learned to shop wisely by accompanying their mothers on expeditions through foreign market places. Young wives who had never before been out of Maine learned that there were other places besides the valley of the Kennebec and more important things to think about than village gossip. The world was wide and varied, they all found, and full of people with viewpoints and customs very different from their own. They learned to understand and accept this, and in so doing broadened and enriched their own lives. The things brought home in the holds of the clippers were valuable; but more valuable were the things brought home in the heads and hearts of the voyagers.

English trade suffered as American trade boomed. To make matters worse, in 1793 France declared war on England. Both sides at once began preying on American shipping for badly needed supplies. The British in addition started stopping American vessels and kidnapping American sailors. They pretended that they were merely recovering British seamen who were evading their patriotic duty by hiding on American ships. Usually the truth was that a British captain was desperate for men to work his vessel, so he took whatever he could lay hands on by any means and regardless of citizenship. England was fighting for her life and could not afford to be too fussy.

To stop this abusive impressment of seamen, Congress passed the Embargo Act of 1807. This forbade trade of any nature with the English, including the Canadians. The new law hit the huge Kennebec fleet hardest of all. Kennebec men complained bitterly; and they acted, too. If they couldn't trade legally, then they'd trade illegally. Almost overnight a navy of expert smugglers and law-evaders came into being.

The British answered the Embargo Act by blockading the whole American coast, except Maine. They thought that perhaps Maine, which had always been a bit independent and self-willed, might prove helpful if her ships were allowed to pass freely. Occasionally English warships even acted as convoys for Maine smugglers, to protect them from search by American patrols. It was a very practical arrangement, although a little irregular.

This was the practice that led to the famous sea fight between the British brig *Boxer* and the American sloop-of-war *Enterprise*, in September of 1813. A group of Kennebec merchants had sent a trading vessel, the *Margaretta*, to New Brunswick for a load of good—although contraband—English wool blankets. The *Boxer* was assigned to escort the *Margaretta* back to home waters to prevent her being captured by other British warships or searched by her own Navy. For a fee of five hundred dollars in gold, the *Boxer*'s captain, William Blythe, agreed to open fire on the merchantman as soon as she entered the wide mouth of the Kennebec. This was to give her a good excuse for not stopping at Customs, where her cargo would need a great deal of explaining.

The plan worked perfectly. Past Fort Popham the *Margaretta* flew, with shot splashing the water all around her. The garrison of the fort, forgetting all about inspection, fired back. The *Boxer* abandoned the pretended chase and put out to sea, and the *Margaretta* proceeded safely up the river with her blankets. And that should have been that, with everybody happy and nobody the worse for wear.

However, some fishing boats nearby heard all the shooting and tore off to Portland, where they knew the *Enterprise* lay. The *Enterprise* had a top fighting reputation, and the fishermen were sure that she would deal properly with anybody who interfered with Kennebec ships. By chance, all the *Enterprise's* older and more responsible officers were off-duty, and she was under the command of Lieutenant William Burrows. He was only twenty-eight years old and had never been under fire. If there had seemed any likelihood of battle action, he would probably not have been left in sole charge.

He was young and eager and spoiling for a fight. When he heard about the firing up near the Kennebec, he couldn't wait to get started. There was no wind and in those days there were no tugboats; but dozens of small craft volunteered to tow him out to

70

Portland Harbor.

sea, where he could catch the slight breeze. The next morning he sighted the *Boxer*, ambling carelessly along off Pemaquid. Her captain, Blythe, was only twenty-nine and just as headlong and full of fight as Burrows. The two ships were evenly matched. Both the young captains evidently considered the encounter more as a sporting event than as a serious and deadly business.

All day long they circled warily. Late in the afternoon they joined battle near Monhegan Island. Almost at once, Blythe lay dead on the deck of his vessel. Within minutes, Burrows was mortally wounded. His men attempted to carry him below, but he commanded them to put him down. He was dying and he knew it; but he swore he would see the British surrender first. It was of no use to argue with him. Instead, the crew fought like fiends. Their guns raked the *Boxer*'s decks and brought down her rigging in a tangle of ropes and splintered wood. Their captain had not long to live, and they intended that his last wish should be fulfilled.

At four o'clock came the hail for which Burrows had been waiting. The officer now in command of the *Boxer* shouted that he had had enough. He was ready to strike his colors and surrender his ship. The dead Blythe's sword was placed in Burrows' shaking hands. "Now I am satisfied," he said. "I die contented."

The *Enterprise*, her flag at half mast, towed the *Boxer* into Portland harbor. The bodies of the two young captains were taken ashore on black-draped barges rowed with muffled oars. Every vessel in port fell in behind in a slow and solemn procession. The bells of Portland tolled, and at one-minute intervals the guns of the fortress thundered. All the people of the city stood with bowed heads along the route of the funeral march. Burrows' coffin was followed by the American seamen, and Blythe's by his own crew. Everybody wept at the death of youth and courage. The two boys were buried side by side in the old cemetery on Munjoy Hill. The stones marking their graves may be seen today standing in the long grass of a sun-dappled knoll overlooking the sea.

This sea fight was partly responsible for bringing British patience with Maine to an end. A strong blockade was enforced along the whole coast, and for a year Kennebec ships collected barnacles and sea slime at their docks. Some trade was conducted between the valley and Boston by oxcart and horse-drawn wagons inching painfully along through dust, mud, or snow over impossible dirt roads. Kennebec humorists referred to this snail-paced procession as the Mud Clipper Fleet or the Horse Marines, but they were not really amused. They knew they faced ruin. They were obliged to sit out the rest of Mr. Madison's War, as the War of 1812 had come to be called. All the while they brooded over the failure of Massachusetts to provide them with protection.

They never regained any faith in Massachusetts. On May 20, 1816, Maine formally seceded from the Commonwealth. The Massachusetts Legislature refused to take this act seriously, and so did Congress in Washington. The Down-Easters took it seriously, though. For four years they existed almost as an independent republic, all the while harassing the higher authorities to pay attention to their arguments. Finally, both Massachusetts and Washington gave in to what had become a nuisance. On March 15, 1820, Maine was at last admitted to the Union as the twenty-third state.

Nine THE BOY FROM SCARBORO

A Kennebec man was largely instrumental in Maine's attaining statehood. He was William King, a fair sample of the caliber of the valley men of the time.

King was born in Scarboro in 1768. He learned that if he was going to amount to anything, it would have to be through his own efforts. There was nobody to help him. When King was seven, his father died almost penniless, leaving to William only a yoke of black oxen. In order to eat and to feed his inheritance, the boy went to work in a sawmill.

He never attended school. To the end of his life, he was unable to spell correctly or speak grammatically. Practical mathematics—the adding of cents into dollars—he learned through necessity. There was nothing the matter with his intelligence or with his ambition.

After a few years, when he was in his teens, King decided that there was no future for him in Scarboro. He had never been able to save the price of a pair of boots; so, barefoot and driving his great black beasts before him, he set out to seek his fortune. Forty miles farther up the coast at Topsham he found a job in a sawmill. It was the only kind of work he knew how to do.

Nobody in Topsham remembered him as the dirty-faced little orphan who could be ignored. Everybody accepted his own rather high rating of himself. By working hard and pinching pennies, William soon owned half a saw, then a whole one, then the mill itself and the timber behind it. Next he bought a store. Now he was really getting into his stride. He added warehouses and wharves to his possessions, and then the ships that landed at the wharves. Six years after his shoeless arrival with his steers, he was filling his own vessels with his own cargoes. Topsham, he now concluded, was getting too small for him. He moved to Bath.

The city was as easy to conquer as Topsham had been. King was one of those Kennebec Yankees who cannot help making money. Soon he owned more stores, warehouses, wharves, and ships. Then he decided that it was cheaper to build ships than to buy them, and he went into the shipbuilding business. His fleet was enormously profitable. One vessel, the *Reunion*, paid for itself three times over in the first three voyages. Then it, along with its sister ships, settled down to providing a large and steady income for the owner.

In King were combined great imagination in business affairs and great ignorance of facts that every schoolboy of today knows. When all his many projects were running smoothly, he looked about for new interests. There were no cotton mills in Maine, because there was no cotton. King saw no reason why raw cotton could not be brought from the South and processed in Maine, where there was plenty of good, cheap water power. He built the first cotton mill in the Province at Brunswick, establishing an industry that continues to the present day. Then he dispatched the *Androscoggin* to New Orleans for a load of cotton.

But when the *Androscoggin*'s captain, Nathaniel Harding, said that he didn't know where New Orleans was, King couldn't help him. He thought maybe it was on the Gulf of Mexico; but, he added, that was not really his problem. It was Harding's. Harding —not very surprisingly—managed to find the Southern port and bring back his cargo. The *Androscoggin* was the first Maine vessel to engage in the cotton trade, which flourished for eighty years.

King had his finger in a score of pies. He bought large tracts of land and went into farming. He raised huge crops of potatoes, which he shipped by his own fleet to the West Indies. He set out five hundred apple trees and sold the fruit profitably in Europe. He was not one to put all his eggs in one basket. Potatoes and apples are to this day the principal Maine agricultural exports.

Not all King's energies were spent in amassing a private fortune. He was public-spirited, too. Through his efforts, the first Maine marine insurance company was founded. He organized the first bank in Bath. The paper currency bore, according to denomination, pictures of the various classes of vessels then in use: schooners, topsail schooners, sloops, brigs, and the like. He backed a law that ended city support of the Congregational church and promoted a toll bridge over the Kennebec. He represented Bath in the General Court of Massachusetts and was made an Honorary General of the Army. All the while he was also working and scheming for the cause of independent statehood.

King had time, in spite of all these activities, for an enjoyable private life. He built himself a mansion on a hill, one of the most elegant and luxurious in all America. It was furnished with the best the world had to offer: mirrors with the gold eagles of France, silver dishes, the candlesticks of emperors, priceless Oriental rugs, rare paintings, and exquisite silk damask draperies. It was a house fit for the entertainment of royalty. In it he entertained the cultural, social, and political leaders of the new America. He entertained well. Through his well-bred and cultivated wife, he acquired gracious manners and a social polish, so that he was at home with his distinguished guests. He had come a long, long way from Scarboro.

The barefoot boy walking behind the slow black oxen on the dusty road to Topsham had dreamed, as all boys do, of wealth and power. Now King—shipbuilder, merchant, landowner, soldier, statesman, and expert in fine living—was wealthy and powerful. It was not enough. Now he had a new ambition, to be the first Governor of Maine. This was the goal toward which he worked. During the War of 1812, he gave generously of both time and money to protect the Maine coast from the British—and to promote the idea of separation from Massachusetts. When statehood became a fact, he was the natural choice for the highest office. He is still referred to as "Maine's first and best Governor."

Originally, Portland was the capital of the new state. A few years later, the seat of government was moved to Augusta. This was sensible. Augusta was more centrally located and in general a more suitable site. So the Kennebec city that started as the fur-trading post of Cushnoc came into its own. It had had a colorful history. For a while, as Fort Western, it served as a buffer between Massachusetts and Canada. With Montcalm's surrender of Quebec, the fort was dismantled and the little settlement around it became part of the town of Hallowell. When the first bridge over the Kennebec was built at the site of the old fort, an independent town called Harrington was incorporated there. Jealous Hallowell citizens persisted in calling the new village Herringtown. This made the Herringtowners so angry they changed the name to Augusta, in honor of the daughter of a Revolutionary hero.

Augusta is by no means the only flourishing Kennebec community to be built on the foundations of a log cabin or rude fishing shack; nor was King the only Kennebec man who ever used the materials at hand to fashion a fine life for himself. But they are both excellent examples and symbols of the spirit of the valley.

Ten KING LOG

Whoever leaves Brunswick by the Bath road passes, even on a bright summer day, into a lovely twilight. The arrowlike rays of the sun slant through lofty white pine tops and dapple a forest floor onto which pine needles have been silently sifting for a thousand years. The trunks of the trees rise seventy feet without a branch. The air is filled with the indescribably clean and heady odor of pine, and with the wind's soft sighing in the arrogant tops far overhead. Many of these trees were standing before the white man ever came to America.

These are the Bowdoin Pines, protected through the foresight of Bowdoin College. They are the pines for which the Vikings sailed west, the mast pines, the pines on which the whole shipbuilding industry of Maine was based. Except for a few small clumps scattered over the state, they are all that are left of the dense pine forest that once covered Maine.

This great natural resource was squandered recklessly. There were hundreds of square miles of the trees, and it seemed as though the supply would never come to an end. Besides, they were in the way. Cornfields and meadows need sunlight and air. The forest giants were cut down to clear the land for farming. The straight-grained wood was ax-hewn into beams for houses and barns, sawn into wide boards for walls and flooring, and split into clapboards and shingles. Pastures were fenced with pine rails, and great quantities of the wood went into boats of all sizes, from a farm boy's little skiff to world-girdling schooners and clippers.

Not all the lumber was used locally. Much of it was sent to England in the form of clapboards, barrel staves, siding, and especially of masts. Special ships were designed to accommodate these enormously long timbers, and great care was taken in their felling to prevent their being warped or broken. All smaller trees were cleared away in the planned line of fall, and a thick bed of saplings, branches, and snow was made to cushion the shock. Once down and limbed out, the masts were dragged to the nearest large watercourse by oxen. Sometimes as many as twenty teams were needed to move one log.

When the ice went out of the Kennebec and the spring freshets came, the logs were herded down toward the sea by crews of river-drivers. It was said of these tough and wiry men that their brains were all in their feet. Agile as cats, they rode the surging, plunging wild wooden horses through snarling rapids and currents as fast as express trains. Their feet thought for themselves as they danced from log to log over gaps of black water. The drivers' business was to keep the timbers moving, to prevent them from being stranded in backwaters or piling up in log jams. Their lives were always in danger of being snuffed out when a foot slipped or one of the giants struck a hidden ledge, lifted twenty feet in the air, and crashed down. The "river-hogs" were experts at their jobs, however, and like most experts, they enjoyed their perilous work.

In the calmer water near the mouth of the river, log booms were strung to catch the winter's cut. The masts were pulled ashore, where they were hand-hewn "sixteen sides." Then they were dragged by oxen to the wharves and loaded onto the ships. Each was worth five hundred dollars, so it is easy to understand why they were nursed along so tenderly. Sometimes they even influenced the map of a town. The peculiar shape of the Common at Freeport was dictated by the need to turn the big sticks here on the route from the lumberyard to the harbor.

When the supply of pine near the coast was gone, the famous Maine lumberjacks went farther and farther up the Kennebec and the other rivers of the state. Gradually the pine forests that had seemed so endless and inexhaustible were nibbled away until today only a few lonely giants rear their heads above the surrounding fir and spruce on the ridges overlooking the upper river. The great days of the mast pines are gone forever.

After the pine vanished, spruce became the important wood. It was not suitable for masts or shipbuilding, but by that time sails had been replaced by steam and wooden hulls by ships of iron. The coarser grain of the spruce was never as beautiful as that of the clear, golden pine, but it was a tough, endurable wood that would take a lot of punishment. Factories and warehouses all over the United States and beyond were floored and roofed with Kennebec spruce, and railroad trains traveled to every part of the country over spruce ties. Spruce was a useful work-a-day wood.

The spruce forests were inland, on the mountainsides of Moosehead and the Rangeley Lakes. This wilderness was largely uninhabited except by deer, moose, wildcats, and bear. The only men who ever went there before the spruce cutting began were an occasional hunter and the gum-gatherers. Armed with long poles tipped with blades, the latter penetrated the spruce belt to fill their knapsacks with the pitch that oozes from the tree to harden into purplish chunks. This by-product of the spruce was the basis of the chewing gum of the day. Americans who had never seen a spruce tree knew the pungent flavor of Kennebec spruce gum.

The spruce loggers were mostly farmers from the lower river

and the French Canadians who were beginning to filter into Maine from the Provinces of Quebec and New Brunswick. Since the timberlands were far from settled areas, logging camps were established in the forest. In November, after the farms had been snugged down for the winter, hundreds of men set off upriver with their packsacks of warm woolen clothes and their axes on their shoulders. They might have to travel a hundred miles, but they got there.

All winter long they worked from sunup until sundown. The woods rang with the sound of axes, the long-drawn cry of "Ti-im-berrr!" and the crash of toppling trees. When the cold northern darkness fell, they gathered in the long bunkhouses, mending clothes and sharpening tools until their early bedtime. It was a monotonous life, mostly hard work with only what little enter-tainment they could provide for themselves by telling stories or listening to the Frenchmen sing. Many learned to knit, or tamed the little chickadees and big, friendly Canadian jays—which they called whiskey-jacks—just for something to do. But it was worth all the boredom. Farmers who had a hard time scratching a living from their stony acres went home with enough money in their pockets to tide them over until the crops came in.

In time, the big spruce went the way of the white pine. The thick stands of the taller trees disappeared. Now came the day of the pulp cutters. Pulpwood is any kind of wood, from scrub spruce and fir to poplar, known in Maine as popple. It is cut into four-foot lengths, rolled onto the ice of streams, and floated down-river when the thaws come. At the mills which have been built along the Kennebec and the Androscoggin, it is ground up and processed into rough paper for newsprint and "pulp" magazines, the better, coated grade for books and "slick" magazines, and top

Logs and papermill at Bucksport, Penobscot Bay.

quality for fine stationery. Kennebec wood still travels all over the world, as it did when it formed the masts of the sailing ships, in the paper of letters, books, and periodicals.

The pulp industry is a mixed blessing for the Kennebec. Nobody questions that paper is a necessity in the reading and writing world of today. The whole operation, from the time the tree stands green on a ridge above the river until the paper comes hot off the rollers of the mills, provides a living for many thousands of people. But a price is paid. Maine's once magnificent forests are being destroyed and her rivers polluted by the waste of the mills. Dyes and chemicals deal death to the bass and shad that once filled Kennebec waters, and a carpet of rotting bark and sawdust covers the feeding grounds and spawning beds of the trout and salmon. The great flocks of fish-eating waterfowl that used to gather in Merrymeeting Bay and along the river can no longer find enough food to support them; and the smaller songbirds that nested on the banks moved away when their leafy cover was poisoned by mill acids.

However, the ruination of the Kennebec Valley is nearing an end. Laws are being drawn up to oblige the mills to dispose of their waste by some other means than dumping it in the river, and reforestation programs are under way. It will take a while to undo the damage; but in time the water will be clear again, the vegetation will recover, schools of fish will nose their inquisitive way up the current, and the wild fowl will return. In time, the Kennebec will again be the lovely river that once it was.

Eleven

One would think that the Kennebec Valley might have escaped being very deeply involved in the Civil War. It was a long way from the Mason-Dixon Line, and not a single slave was owned in the area. Many of the people living there had never even seen a Negro. A fair share of men and of money would be contributed toward the preserving of the Union, of course. But aside from that, it would seem offhand that Kennebec citizens need not be seriously affected.

This was not the case. Through the cotton trade, a strong bond had been cemented between the Valley and the South. It was said that Bath and New Orleans were closer neighbors than Richmond, Virginia, and Washington, D.C. Except geographically, this was true. Ships bound for the Mississippi city left the mouth of the Kennebec almost daily and returned with their holds full of cotton bales. Many Southern businessmen owned shares in these vessels and in the mills; and many Maine men had money invested in Southern enterprises.

True friendships of fifty years' standing arose out of these partnerships. They led to much visiting back and forth. The distance was great, but it was always easy to arrange for comfortable transportation on a trade ship. Captains frequently took their wives and children along on the voyages. Boys and girls from Brunswick and Hallowell played almost as often under magnolia trees with Southern children as they did with the neighborhood children under the elms of home. In time, many of them grew up

84

to marry. In spite of the long sea-miles between their birthplaces, they knew and understood each other well. They had grown up together. Very often a Yankee groom would build his Southern bride a house where she would feel truly at home. That is why there are so many Southern mansions with their overhanging porticos and Greek columns in the towns along the Kennebec.

These close ties of friendship and kinship could not be broken without a great deal of heartache. Men who had interests in the South were suddenly viewed with dark suspicion by their Kennebec neighbors. It was felt that they could not be trusted, and their local businesses fell away to nothing. The lovely Southern belles who had been so gay and popular were snubbed and shunned by Kennebec society. They sat alone and lonely in their plantation-style mansions, homesick in the bleak, unfriendly climate for the warm, easygoing land of their birth. Many of these men and women never regained their lost happiness. They were war victims as surely as the soldiers who fell at Bull Run.

Lost money sounds less romantic than lost happiness. Nevertheless, it is hard to see almost everything you possess abruptly destroyed. That is what happened to most of the Kennebec shipowners. Four days after the firing on Fort Sumter, the Confederacy began issuing letters of marque and reprisal. These are documents carried by ships' captains giving them authority to seize the merchant ships of an enemy power. They encourage what amounts to legalized piracy.

The shipowners should have expected this and prepared for it by arming their vessels, but they did not. As a result, hundreds of Maine vessels were captured by Southern privateers almost immediately. Less than a year later, Kennebec shipping was practically wiped out. It seemed doubtful whether it would ever

The Nickels-Sortwell House, Wiscasset.

again flourish. With shipping at a standstill, the mills suffered equally from a lack of raw materials.

In addition, the valley was making the expected contributions of men and money. Maine as a whole gave eighteen million dollars, a huge sum for so small a state. She also sent off to battle over ten percent of her entire population. One of her regiments is given the credit for saving the Union line at Gettysburg. This was the Twentieth Regiment Infantry, Maine Volunteers. Many, many Kennebec boys served in the Twentieth Maine, as it was called.

The Twentieth was a typical Maine regiment. It was made up of men and boys from isolated farms and small villages. None of them had the faintest notion of military discipline at first. They didn't even carry themselves or behave like soldiers. When they received an order, they were just as apt as not to ask "Why?" The officers—who were Maine men, too, and understood the Maine way of operating—were perfectly willing to explain and if necessary to argue. If the order then seemed reasonable, it was obeyed. If not, both men and officers squatted on their heels or leaned against trees with their hands in their pockets while they talked the matter over. When they had all agreed on a good course of action, they at last carried out the revised order.

This casual assembly was commanded by Colonel Adelbert Ames. Ames came from Maine, but he had been trained at West Point. He had also been awarded the Congressional Medal of Honor for outstanding bravery at the first Battle of Bull Run. With all this military training and experience behind him, he knew what a body of fighting men ought to look like. When he first laid eyes on his new command, he was completely disgusted. "This is a hell of a regiment," he said. Eleven months later, in July of 1863, he stood on the rolling fields at Gettysburg and watched the thin, tough line of the Twentieth Maine stand unwavering under attack after attack. "This is a hell of a *regiment!*" he said again. This time there was only great respect and pride in his tone.

Lincoln's Vice President during the Civil War was a Kennebec Valley man. No one along the Little Androscoggin was surprised at this. They had all been expecting something of the sort for fifty years, since 1809. During that winter, an Indian squaw known as Molly Ockett had started to walk from Andover to Paris. She was one of the few remaining of the local tribe, who wandered around the region in a rather lost manner. Everyone knew her. Some thought she was crazy, some considered her a witch, most had great faith in the medicines she brewed from herbs and roots, and everyone agreed that she was harmless.

Part way to her destination, Molly Ockett was overtaken by a blizzard. There was a mill at Snow Falls, on the Little Androscoggin, and there she asked for shelter. The miller was new in the district. He didn't know Molly or the fact that she was always made welcome everywhere. He was probably afraid of Indians. At any rate, he turned her away. She was furious. She cursed him, his whole family, and the very earth beneath the mill. Nothing, she swore, would ever prosper on that plot of ground.

Then she turned her outraged back on the surly miller and continued her struggle along the snow-drifted road. Finally she arrived at the hamlet of Paris Hill, where she found refuge in a modest farmhouse. She was seated by the fire and given a good hot meal. As she ate, the young housewife sat beside her holding a sick baby. When Molly was warmed through and comfortably full, she took the child in her arms and crooned to him. He would be all right, she assured the anxious mother. What was more, he would grow up to become a famous man, well-known and re-

Harriet Beecher Stowe.

pected in faraway places by many many people.

Nobody, therefore, found cause for amazement when Hannibal Hamlin became the twenty-third Governor of Maine, then a United States Senator, and finally, in 1861, the Vice President of the United States.

Nobody was much surprised either when the mill at Snow Falls burned down shortly after Molly Ockett put her curse on it. It does seem a little odd, though, that in the century and a half since the miller refused her shelter, nothing has succeeded at Snow Falls. Several projects have been attempted there, but all have failed. This is a little hard to explain, unless you believe in Indian curses.

A Kennebec woman was largely responsible for the strong feeling against slavery in the North. She was Harriet Beecher Stowe, the wife of a Brunswick minister. One Sunday, her husband was puzzled to see her rise and leave the church in the middle of his sermon. She said later that a vision suddenly appeared before her, more real and vivid than the worshippers around her. It showed an old Negro dying from the lashing of a slave overseer, while a beautiful golden-haired child looked down from Heaven. Mrs. Stowe went home and at once started writing *Uncle Tom's Cabin.* Thousands of people read this perhaps one-sided account of the abuse of slaves and were stirred to anger. Today we would probably call such a book a piece of propaganda. Be that as it may, it aroused violent public sentiment that without doubt helped bring on the war.

Twelve

After the Civil War, things were bad along the Kennebec. With the mills idle, there was not much to export in what remained of the merchant marine. Often the ships had to sail with empty holds. An empty ship is an unmanageable ship, floating high in the water, the victim of any wind stronger than a light breeze. To overcome this top-heaviness, something has to be used as ballast. Lacking anything alse, the shipowners started using ice, which was both plentiful and cheap—an important consideration. Thus, by accident, was born the industry that was to lift the area out of the depression.

For the captains discovered to their delighted surprise that ice, which was almost worthless at home, could be sold at a good profit in the tropics, the semi-tropics, the South and abroad. At once, almost everyone in the valley became an iceman.

Kennebec Yankees are shrewd. They passed the word around the world that Kennebec ice was purer, clearer, longer-lasting and in every way better than any other ice. Today this would be called a promotion campaign. Actually, this boasted superiority was imaginary. The Kennebec was unpolluted, it was true; but so were most rivers at that time, and their ice was just as clean, safe, and solid. It pays to advertise, however. Soon Kennebec ice became the ice in demand and commanded a higher price than any other.

As would be expected, unprincipled businessmen elsewhere took advantage of this fact. In New York and London, in Paris and Alabama, in Hong Kong, Cairo, and Manila, in Cuba and in the dusty villages amid the cornlands of Nebraska, wagons had painted in large letters on their sides "Kennebec Ice." This was the magic ice, the ice that could be depended on to turn out the firmest ice cream in hand-operated freezers, that tinkled most musically in tall pitchers of lemonade, that lasted longest in zinc-lined wooden iceboxes, that chilled fruits and salads most perfectly. This was the ice everybody preferred.

In reality, much of it never saw the Kennebec or even Maine. A great deal of it came from the Hudson. One New York ice company handled a large part of the Kennebec crop. It also used the Hudson as a source of supply. One block of ice looks very much like another, so it was easy for the company's employees to get them mixed up, and convenient, too. What people didn't know, they reasoned, wouldn't hurt them. It probably didn't.

Preparations for the ice harvest started along the Kennebec well before Christmas. The cavernous icehouses down by the river, for months shut and silent except for the thin buzzing of wasps, were opened. Last year's musty sawdust, used as insulation to prevent melting, was cleared out. The sections of track over which the ice was conveyed into the storage building were rubbed free of rust, and the machinery was overhauled. Horses were sharp-shod with calks of steel, and cutting tools were honed to fine edges. Everything was ready and waiting for a good cold snap to start things moving.

From New Year's on, everyone along the river watched his thermometer like a hawk. If unseasonably mild weather continued, storekeepers in large towns and small villages alike shook their heads. They didn't have to consult their ledgers to know that the columns of debts were growing longer and longer. Riding about the countryside behind their patient mares, doctors performed their services without fee. Farmers watched the level of the cattle feed drop in the big bins and wondered where the money to buy more would come from. Their wives took to skimping on sugar and making one-egg cakes instead of two. Teachers in little red schoolhouses grew short with their pupils as they worried about their pay. In the gracious mansions overlooking the river, the owners and the captains of the ice vessels fretted. In these hard times, everyone in the valley depended directly or indirectly on the ice crop.

Once in a great while, Maine experienced a comparatively warm, open winter, and the ice industry suffered accordingly. Usually, however, the bitter cold came. At dusk the sky was clear, and a knife-edged wind blew out of the northwest. The mercury in the thermometers dropped steadily. The pines roared in the dark beneath the brilliant stars. After midnight, the wind fell and it became still as a pocket. Frost ferns grew slowly on the panes of kitchen windows. In the morning, the water in the buckets by the sink was skimmed over, and the river lay like a long black mirror between the hills.

The zero weather continued for the next night and the next. Each morning the river was blacker. Water expands as it freezes. As the ice thickened, it yielded to the pressure, cracking with an eerie howl that echoed and re-echoed far up through the hills. On the fourth afternoon, the river suddenly blossomed with children in bright caps, scarfs, and mittens, just out of school. They were joined by young men and women, and older ones, too, from the farms and villages. Everybody who could stand up was on skates, cutting figure eights, doing outer edges, playing snap-the-whip and fox-and-geese. At night bonfires flamed along the banks of the river from above Augusta all the way to the sea.

A day or two later, the ice was thick enough to bear the weight of horses and sleighs, and the Kennebec became a highway connecting all the river towns. Sleighs piled high with buffalo robes flew up and down, the bells of the harnesses merry in the frosty air. The ice was marked off into lanes, and races were organized. Along these tracks the horses came, neck and neck, the vapor of their breaths streaming white behind them and diamond chips flying from beneath their iron-shod hooves. For a few days it was like a carnival, breaking the long monotony of the winter with something gay and charming.

Then the ice was thick enough to cut. The fun ended and the work began. Farmers from the entire valley and drifters from all over New England and beyond crowded the river lodging houses of Hallowell, Brunswick, Gardiner, and Dresden. They dressed themselves warmly in thick wools, armed themselves with picks, gougers, saws, and cantdogs, and hired themselves out to help harvest this seasonal crop. It was a chance to make a little money at a time of year when no other work was available.

Ice cutting was hard, cold labor. First the area to be cut was marked off into squares, like a gigantic pan of fudge. This was done with the gougers, both manhandled and horse-drawn. Then the sawyers came with their long saws. They stood with both hands on one end of their long tools, pushing down, pulling up, over and over and over. Sawyers could be spotted on sight by their magnificent shoulder muscles.

At noon everyone went ashore to the fires that had been built on the banks. They warmed their hands and feet and dug into their packages of thick sandwiches, frosty doughnuts, and apple pie. Then they lighted their pipes or bit off a chew of tobacco and relaxed for a few minutes before returning to work.

During the afternoon, the ice cut in the morning had to be seen safely into the icehouses. Otherwise it would freeze back into place and a whole morning's work would be wasted. With cantdogs and picks, the hundred-pound blocks were heaved out of the water and skidded across the solid ice to the runways. Chains clanked, hooks bit into them, and they flashed along the rails like huge emeralds. With a crash they plunged into the great sheds, where men caught them and piled them to the right and left. Gradually the walls of ice rose until they reached the roof. At last, even the central aisle between the cakes was filled, and sawdust was heaped over all. Then the big doors were closed and sealed. Ice harvesting was done for another year.

Now everyone in the valley could draw a breath of relief. Now the storekeeper and the doctor could be paid out of wallets fat with ice cutting wages. The grain bin and flour barrel were full again, and teachers regained their patience. The owners and the captains stopped worrying about their vessels sailing with empty holds. All was fine again along the Kennebec.

The ice-exporting business flourished up into the twentieth century. Then it had to give way to modern methods of refrigeration. Now very little ice is cut in Maine except by private individuals for their own use. The big icehouses have rotted down, and the rusty tools are regarded as interesting antiques. Children on hot city streets no longer run after the red ice wagon to beg a sliver of Kennebec ice to suck. Many young people of today, accustomed to the cloudy cubes of machine-made ice, have never known how crystal-clear pond or river ice can be. Perhaps the irregular splinters were not really colder than modern ice, but they seemed colder.

Short-lived as it was, however, the ice industry served the Kennebec country well. It tided the whole area over what could have been a disastrous period of depression.

Thirteen

For almost a thousand years, ever since the Vikings came to the Maine coast for lumber, the Kennebec has exported a great variety of things to all parts of the world. The valley has been like a huge storehouse out of which came furs and fish, sassafras root and spruce gum, apples and ice, woolen and cotton fabrics, masts, paper, and barrel staves. During the French and Indian Wars, there was for a short time a lively trade in scalps, which were bought as curiosities abroad. They were priced at anywhere between five and a hundred dollars, depending. Naturally, the scalp of an outstanding Abenaki chief was worth more than that of some ordinary little brave that nobody had ever heard of.

For a while, cobblestones were an important export. The seaward beaches around the mouth of the river and on the exposed islands are composed of stones about the size of ostrich eggs. They look like ostrich eggs, too, having been smoothed and shaped by the terrific action of the surf. These made perfect cobbles, and they were free for the taking. Ships carried them to all parts of the United States and to Europe, where they were used to pave city streets. They made a very durable, but rough, pavement. When automobiles replaced horse-drawn carriages and drays, most of the streets were resurfaced. In a few places, however, where history and tradition are valued, stretches of the old Kennebec cobbles are preserved as reminders of the past. There are some on Beacon Hill in Boston, and in Alexandria, Virginia.

The same shrewdness that enabled Kennebec men to see possibilities in worthless stones showed them how to use another product of the outer beaches. This is driftwood, great quantities of which are washed ashore by the winter storms. Old driftwood is no good for building and not much good for firewood, except on picnics. But it is often very beautiful. The salt and sun bleach the oddly shaped sections of trees and deeply grained planking of wrecked boats to a soft silver-gray, and the sea smooths and polishes the surfaces. A market has been developed for these natural works of art. The larger pieces are sold to decorate the lobbies of hotels and public buildings or the display windows of department stores. Smaller pieces are made into lamps, coffee tables, and other furniture. There are people along the coast who make several thousand dollars a year in a business that boils down to the pleasant occupation of walking along the shore, picking up sticks.

The material objects that have flowed out of the valley have had value; but perhaps the most valuable of all the Kennebec exports was something entirely different, something that could be neither bought nor sold: people and ideas. The two are impossible to separate. There are people without an idea in their heads; but there has never been an idea that didn't start with a person. Something about the Kennebec valley seems to have encouraged ideas. It was, rather surprisingly, the place where the automotive industry began. The records tell us that Henry Alonzo House built the first successful steam automobile in 1866, in Bridgeport, Connecticut. Actually, there was a workable steam automobile running around Gardiner eight years before that.

Some of the ideas have been less practical. That of Captain Samuel Clough of Wiscasset is a good example. Captain Clough was a hard-fisted, level-headed Yankee skipper who had sailed his

98

A cobblestone street in Boston.

merchantman, the *Sally*, over much of the world. In 1793, he and the *Sally* somehow became involved in an improbable scheme to save Queen Marie Antoinette of France from the guillotine. There are two theories as to why he lent himself and his ship to such a very dangerous enterprise. Some romantic people think that his heart was touched by the plight of the unhappy Queen, and that he acted out of pure chivalry. Others believe that he was hired to carry her to America, that the whole thing was a business arrangement. The latter seems the more likely, since Yankee sea captains were always alert for opportunities to make a dollar. In either case, he was risking his ship and his life by joining the plot.

The plan went further than just rescuing Marie Antoinette. Captain Clough's idea was that she should find shelter in his home in Wiscasset. He wrote his wife "to prepare to receive not a queen, but only a very sad and broken-hearted lady." How Mrs. Clough took the news that she was about to entertain royalty we have no way of knowing. We can guess, though. She was a plain Kennebec housewife, hardworking and matter-of-fact. She could not have been overjoyed at the prospect of having her whole routine upset by this pampered French aristocrat. She probably did not especially appreciate having her husband risk life and limb for another woman, queen or no queen, either. She undoubtedly wondered what to feed a royal guest. Would she be satisfied with good fish chowder and johnnycake, or would she expect fancy French cooking? Poor Mrs. Clough must have spent some uneasy moments.

Her husband, meanwhile, was making his own preparations for the comfort of the refugee. So that she would feel at home on the bleak Maine coast, he smuggled aboard his ship all sorts of luxuries. There was a whole wardrobe of beautiful clothes; and

100

furniture, draperies, and rugs for the rooms intended for her. There was exquisite china and silver to enhance her table, and priceless bric-a-brac to delight her eye. He even loaded rolls of lovely French wallpaper to adorn her quarters. The Queen was at the time a prisoner in her own palace, so all these articles had to be spirited out under the noses of the guards. If the captain had been caught—but he wasn't.

Not quite. There was a sudden uprising, during which Marie Antoinette was seized and imprisoned, eventually to be beheaded. Captain Clough was warned in time to slip anchor and make his getaway, but not in time to unload the royal belongings. They sailed with him to Wiscasset, where for a long while they were stored in the attic of the house. Perhaps Captain Clough considered himself only a caretaker of the valuable property; or perhaps Mrs. Clough thought the things were too fancy for everyday living.

Time went by, and nobody came to claim the cargo. Gradually it was put to use. An elaborate satin robe worn by the King of France on state occasions was made over into a Sunday-go-to-meeting dress for Mrs. Clough. When the kitchen clock wore out, a lovely clock presented to Marie Antoinette on her son's birthday took its place on the shelf over the sink. When the Cloughs died, everything was auctioned off. Some pieces are now in the Metropolitan Museum of Art in New York. Most of the rest are scattered around among the homes of the lower Kennebec. The delicate gilded chairs, brightly enameled snuffboxes, and fragile china statuettes are reminders of a fantastic idea that almost worked.

In 1793, the same year that Captain Clough tried to rescue the Queen of France, a small group of people with an idea of their

101

own drifted into the Kennebec Valley. They were members of a religious group known as the Shakers. Their beliefs were outlined in a long and complicated Covenant. The whole thing, however, was based on a simple idea: to be good. This is what most religions teach: that it is better to be good than to be bad. What made the Shakers different was that they tried much harder than almost anyone else.

In some places the Shakers had been treated as crackpots. In others they had been suspected of all sorts of terrible things, just because they were different. People along the Kennebec have a tendency toward minding their own business and letting others mind theirs. This was all that the Shakers wanted. They started a community at Sabbathday Lake in the rolling hills overlooking the Little Androscoggin. One of the Shaker beliefs was that hard work was a fine thing. The Kennebec farmers believed this, too. In no time at all, they were viewing their new neighbors with a great deal of respect and liking. Soon many of the local people joined the community.

When a member was accepted, he turned over all his property to the community and went to live in one of the big stone buildings on the high ridge above the lake. He could, however, change his mind and leave with his belongings at any time. Very few did this. The community was a busy, happy place, where each person worked at what best suited him. Almost nowhere else could anyone find a pleasanter or more satisfying life.

The Shakers did not believe in marriage. To assure the future of the community, they adopted orphaned, abandoned, or unwanted children of the area. These were free to leave when they became of age. Most of them stayed, and of those who left, many returned. Nowhere in the outside world could they find the atmosphere of peace and loving-kindness that existed at Sabbathday. Within a few decades, between the joinings and the adoptions, the membership of the community consisted largely of people with Kennebec roots.

They were mostly country people who loved animals and plants. Under their care the fields and orchards, and the flocks and herds flourished. The farmers at Shaker Village conducted agricultural experiments far in advance of the times and produced many good hybrids. They packaged the seeds of the best selected strains and sold them about the countryside. These were the first packaged, labeled, and guaranteed seeds in the whole history of agriculture. That alone makes the Shakers worth remembering.

Kennebec Yankees have always been of an inventive turn of mind. This came to full flower in Shaker Village, where everyone worked without pressure. Altogether the Shakers are credited with almost a hundred inventions. They include such common and supposedly modern articles as the circular saw, the rotary harrow, Babbit metal, flat brooms, metal pens, condensed milk, and wrinkle-proof and water-repellent cloth. Since Shakers believed ideas should belong to everybody, they never had any of their inventions patented. It was left to other later inventors to profit from them.

There is still a Shaker Village at Sabbathday Lake. It is very small now. Today welfare agencies take care of the waifs and strays that used to find shelter there. So the massive stone buildings looking down over the orchards and meadows are almost empty, monuments to a rather impractical idea that actually did work.

A great many sons and daughters of the Kennebec have gone out to make their mark in the world. Almost always they have carried with them the stamp of their valley. A good example is Mellie Dunham, a snowshoe maker of Norway, on the banks of the Little Androscoggin. Besides making snowshoes, Mellie farmed a few acres up on Crockett's Ridge, hunted and fished a little, and played his fiddle at the local square dances. Until he was over seventy, the only thing that set him apart from a thousand other men of the valley was the fact that Admiral Robert E. Peary was wearing a pair of Dunham snowshoes when he discovered the North Pole. The Admiral sent Mellie a walrus hide and a note of appreciation; and the snowshoes with Mellie Dunham's name burned into the frame may be seen today at the Smithsonian Institution in Washington, D.C.

When he was seventy-two, Mellie entered a fiddling contest in Lewiston, held to choose the Champion Fiddler of Maine. He didn't take fiddling seriously, but he thought it might be fun to hear the other fellers play. To his own great surprise, he won the contest. A few weeks later, as he was looking through his mail, he remarked to his wife Emma, "I see there's a letter here from Henry."

"Henry who?" Emma asked. She couldn't think of any Henry who might be writing to Mellie.

"Henry Ford," Mellie told her. "What other Henry is there?"

Ford was conducting a contest to find America's champion old-time fiddler, and he was inviting Mellie to come out to Dearborn, expenses paid, to compete. Mellie decided to go. He'd never been outside Maine, and if he was ever going to go, now seemed the time. With his old fiddle and a pair of special snowshoes for Henry, he set forth. The whole Kennebec country turned out to give him a send-off. Along the Kennebec, where almost every farmer owned or had owned a Model T or a Model A, Henry

Ford was a far more important person than all the kings of Europe rolled into one.

Mellie didn't take the competition very seriously. He wore the clean khaki pants and gray work shirt that served him as fiddling-clothes at the dances back home. He played as he had always played, sawing away like mad, stamping time with his off foot, and swearing mildly under his breath. With his halo of white hair on end, he ripped through "Turkey in the Straw" and "Boston Fancy." He was having a wonderful time, and that was all that mattered. When everyone stood up and cheered him, he was, as they say along the Kennebec, flabbergasted. He couldn't believe that he was the Champion Old-time Fiddler of the United States.

He couldn't believe it either when an entertainment circuit offered him five hundred dollars a week for bookings in their theaters for the entire winter. That amounted to more money than he had actually handled in half a lifetime. He thought there must be some mistake. "I ain't no artist," he warned. "I'm just an old country fiddler from Norway, Maine." They wanted him just the same.

He was a great success with audiences everywhere. He had no act at all. He simply got up there and played as though he were back at a Kennebec barn dance. Everybody loved him, and he could have gone on year after year, making money and living an exciting life. But he was seventy-three years old, and he was getting tired. It had all been real interesting, and folks had certainly been nice to him, but he wanted to go home.

So back he went to Crockett's Ridge and stayed there for the rest of his life. He'd accomplished quite a lot at that, for an up-river farmer. His snowshoes had been to the roof of the world, his music had gladdened countless hearts, and he himself—by simply being plain Mellie Dunham—had served as one of the best ambassadors the Kennebec ever had.

There have been many others—too many to list. There was Edwin Arlington Robinson, one of America's greatest poets, who was born at Head Tide, near Gardiner. The scenes and acquaintances of his boyhood are reflected in his work. One of his poems, *Richard Cory*, has even been made into a ballad that is sung by groups of young modern folk singers. It makes a very good folk song.

Then there is Margaret Chase Smith, born in Skowhegan, the first woman ever to be elected to the United States Senate solely on her own merits. She is also the first woman ever to run for the Presidency of the nation. Although she is a small, quiet woman, the other members of the Senate sit up and pay attention when the Kennebec's Mrs. Smith speaks.

There is one other export of the valley on which a price tag cannot be tied. That is words—not words written in books, but the live words of everyday speech. The Kennebec has a language of its own. It is a language that springs from the daily occupations of the people along the river, of the offshore islands and on the farms back in the hills. Instead of calling a person prim and proper, Kennebec folk say that butter wouldn't melt in his mouth. Flattery is called buttering up. A spoiled child is the white hen's chicken. A family that is short of money has rough sledding or a hard row to hoe. A proud man goes with head up and tail over the dashboard. He's as independent as a hog on ice. Those are country sayings.

From the coast come phrases with the flavor of the old sailing days about them. When a self-important woman enters a public gathering, she is sometimes described as tacking in under a full spread of canvas. A discouraged man may say that he has come to the bitter end, which means to the last few feet of rope on a windlass bitt. A person who has lost everything he owns is stripped to bare poles, as a clipper might be after a typhoon. Anybody in difficulties is close-hauled. If he fails to surmount his troubles, to weather the gale, he is said to be on his beam ends, as a wrecked ship rests on the ends of the beams used in her construction.

Along the river, an ill person looks like the last run of shad. Some people are slippery as eels and some have as many faces as the town clock. An unexpected visitor has come down on the drive, an expression that refers to log drives of olden days. There are those who are as homely as hedge fences, those who are as cheerful as baskets of chips, and those who are as bright as crickets.

Some of these expressions are familiar everywhere, even though they originated in the valley. When the Kennebec Yankees moved west in their covered wagons or east in their sailing vessels, they took with them more than could be seen or touched. They carried on the tips of their tongues truly imperishable heirlooms to be handed down from generation to generation of their descendants.

Fourteen

After the Civil War, the history of the Kennebec ran parallel to the history of the rest of the country. Men from the valley fought in the same wars as men from California. They voted in the same national elections, furnished their homes with the same modern conveniences, and drove the same models of cars over the same kind of improved highways. Their children were moved from the little old one-room schoolhouses into big, centralized consolidated schools, with their better facilities. In general, the river kept abreast of changing times.

For a while, there were even railroads with trains trundling every day all the way up past Skowhegan and Rumford, halting in a leisurely manner at whistle-stops and milk-stops to pick up passengers and the big milk cans. The trains were fun. Everybody knew everybody else and the conductors acted more like hosts than like officials. But the passenger trains are gone now. People ride on buses or in their own cars. Along the Kennebec, and indeed in all of Maine, there are now only occasional freight trains.

But the valley really hasn't changed as much as might be imagined. Kennebec people were never ones to veer like weathervanes in the slightest breeze. The rest of the world might become standardized, but never them. They adapted, but they adapted slowly and with reservations. They clung to the old until it was proven without doubt that the new was better. Sometimes they never became convinced; and some things can never be changed.

108

An eight-hour day and a five-day week are fine, but they don't work very well if, as so many men do on the Kennebec, you farm or fish for a living. Cattle and codfish have not yet heard about time clocks and labor laws.

Kennebec farms are small, so small and so stony and tip-tilted that it is not practical to install expensive milking machines or enormous harvesting combines. Cows are milked by hand, and fields are usually plowed and harrowed by horse-drawn equipment, although some farmers have at last overcome their distrust of newfangled notions enough to buy small tractors. But by and large, a Kennebec farm is an old-fashioned farm.

One thing has changed. In the old days, each farm raised a great variety of crops, much of which was stored or home-canned to feed the family throughout the winter. Today there are several large commercial canning companies in Maine. They depend on the surrounding area for produce. Agents of the companies call on the farmers during the winter and arrange with them what crop each shall plant. The company furnishes the seed and agrees to buy the harvest at a prearranged price. This gives the farmers greater security than they once had, and more ready cash for store-bought groceries.

It also provides the children with a chance to earn a little money of their own. When the stringbeans, for example, are ready to be picked, they must be picked right away, before they pass their peak of goodness. Then the beanfields blossom with sunburned boys and blue-jeaned girls, busy as beavers as they work their way down the long rows. In picking season when the weather looks threatening, schools are often closed until the crop is in. Picking beans is not the easiest work in the world, but almost any valley child would rather be outdoors than in school. Usually a

Engine and cars of the railroad between Old Orchard and the Saco River.

---

prize is given to the one who turns in the most bushels of beans. This makes the whole thing into a game.

Of recent years, Kennebec farmers have been harvesting a new crop, Christmas trees. The demand comes at just the right time of year, when there isn't much to do around the farm except tend the livestock. In November, the Christmas tree cutters—the farmers, their sons, and their fishermen neighbors—go into abandoned back pastures and old pulp slashes that are springing up to second- and third-growth spruce and fir. Soon the roadsides are high-walled with bundles of the evergreen trees. They range in size from two-foot table trees, through family trees of six or eight feet, up to thirty- or forty-foot giants for hotel lobbies and municipal parks.

Early in December, trucks start picking them up and heading

south and west with their green, aromatic loads for Boston, New York, Philadelphia, and beyond. Everyone who owns a truck and can possibly spare it goes into the business of hauling Christmas trees. There are so many that the Maine Turnpike Authority puts up special signs during the season: "Christmas Tree Trucks Use Outer Lane." It's rather nice to think of all these lovely trees scattered far and wide through cities and towns, bringing the pungent scent of Kennebec balsam into homes hundreds of miles away from the river.

While the men and boys are busy cutting and hauling the trees, the farm girls and women are occupied, too, making Christmas wreaths. This is a real business, even though it is carried on in the kitchens of farms and fishing shacks. Before the snow comes, the children go into the woods and gather sacks of ground pine and small fir and spruce branches. This is heaped in barns and sheds, where the cold will keep it fresh and green. A few weeks before Christmas, the girls and women start making wreaths which will be carried by trucks to the cities. The kitchens are filled with the spicy smell of the evergreens, released by the heat of the wood-burning stoves to mingle with the mouth-watering odors of coffee and fresh-baked bread. A good worker can make four or five wreaths an hour. At about thirty cents a wreath, it adds up to a goodly sum for holiday spending. It's almost like money found on the forest floor.

The very first people along the Kennebec were hunters, and there have been many hunters there ever since. Nowadays, while many of them are valley natives who simply do a little hunting in their off-time, many more come from far places during the season for the sole purpose of hunting. Merrymeeting Bay is now considered to be one of the best duck-hunting regions on the entire

Atlantic seaboard. In 1890, a Captain Samuel Nickerson started planting wild rice there to attract migrating waterfowl. This was so successful that the State Inland Fish and Game Commission took over the project. As a result, the Bay is a duck-hunter's paradise. Sportsmen come from all over to shoot there.

Deer-hunters come too, to stay at the hunting lodges up in the mountains around Moosehead and the Rangeley Lakes, or in the homes of farmers. They roam the November woods in their bright jackets and caps, imagining themselves to be modern-day Daniel Boones. The Kennebec farmer-fishermen-lumberjacks add another to their list of occupations. They now become licensed guides to the out-of-state hunters, helping them to find game and preventing them from getting lost in what in many places remains pathless wilderness. The hunting season is a busy and stimulating time for everyone.

Autumn is not the only season for visitors from other places. In the last thirty or forty years, Maine as a whole has become popular as a vacation area—so much so that the license plates of cars bear the word *Vacationland*. The whole great basin drained by the Kennebec benefits from this. It has so much to offer, something to suit the taste of almost everyone. Down by the mouth of the river are the sea-beaches and the little unspoiled islands. Further upstream is pleasant countryside dotted with a thousand crystal-clear lakes. And far up where the river begins is the wild country of mountain and deep forest. It's a wonderful land in which to entertain guests, like a mansion of many differently furnished rooms.

The coming of tourists in such large numbers has naturally changed the valley. Tourism is now actually a business. The state has spent a great deal of money on good roads and attractive rest

Unspoiled islands in the mouth of the Kennebec River.

areas to make travel easy. Motels and gift shops have sprung up, and a great many farmhouses and comfortable small-town homes bear signs, "Tourists Accommodated." There are special attractions for the visitors—summer theaters, art exhibits, and deep-sea fishing trips, for example. They all add to the prosperity of the region.

All this is not as cold-blooded as it sounds. In the days of the clipper ships, sons and daughters of the Kennebec were familiar with every port and every country in the world. They came home with their heads full of new ideas and new viewpoints. Now the world comes to the Kennebec, bringing fresh attitudes and opinions. The result is the same in both cases—a broadening of minds and a growth of knowledge and tolerance among the stay-at-homes. Very often summer visitors return year after year to a place in which they have found something peaceful and good for which they have been looking. Then what started as a business relationship becomes a real and lasting friendship to which both sides contribute. The tourists bring more than money to the valley.

There are other newcomers along the Kennebec; but these have come to stay. They are the French-Canadians from the Province of Quebec. At first there were only a few handfuls of men working here and there in the winter lumbercamps. Then more came with their families to find employment in the cotton and paper mills of Brunswick, Waterville, Lewiston, and Rumford. In the beginning they lived in small houses crowded together in the poorer sections. Every Kennebec and Androscoggin city and village had its Frenchtown. The quick, dark, excitable Canucks, as they were called, were looked down upon by the taller, blue-eyed Yankees.

114

They didn't seem to care much. They kept to themselves. They spoke to each other in their own lively, explosive tongue, cooked according to their own taste, had their own schools, their own barbershops and bakeries, and their own Catholic churches. They dressed oddly, but with great style; laughed a lot and argued a lot; and had enormous families. They were good workers and great savers, making every penny buy the value of three.

Shortly the thrifty Canucks began to move into the better houses. Some of them acquired run-down or abandoned farms. With their usual energy and enthusiasm, they set about repairing tumbled stone walls, repainting shabby buildings and restoring worn-out fields. Long neglected orchards once again bore fruit, and meadows grown up to hawkweed and juniper once again grazed sheep and cattle. By this time, the Yankees had become used to the Canucks. The general opinion was that the Frenchmen weren't so bad, once you got to know them. They had their little peculiarities; but then, who hadn't?

Today some stores in Kennebec cities have notices in their windows, "On parle Francais ici"—French spoken here. Some newsstands sell French-language Quebec and Montreal papers. Sometimes, walking down a street, you hear a ripple of French conversation or a burst of gayer-than-Yankee laughter. Otherwise there is no way of telling that two groups of widely different backgrounds and temperament inhabit the valley. Both French- and English-descended men practice medicine and law, hold public office, teach school, and conduct businesses. Their families intermarry. They are all Americans who happen to live along the Kennebec.

The valley is full of contrasts that manage to get along together. Far back in the hills of Oxford County where the Androscoggin has its beginnings is the tiny village of Andover. There are a couple of general stores, a Post Office, a schoolhouse and a church in Andover, and fifty or sixty houses strung along the few short streets that end in thick woods. Often during winter storms the telephone lines are down, and it is impossible to call up your next-door neighbor. Once in a while ten-foot drifts of hard-packed snow block the only road out of town, and not even the mail can get through. The place is completely isolated for a while.

Yet up in a huge bowl-like valley in the hills only a mile or so from the center of the hamlet, men are talking directly with Europe by means of a satellite in space. When experiments with direct overseas telephone and television transmission were begun, Andover was chosen for the first Telstar Earth Station. Sending and receiving conditions were discovered to be ideal there. There were no large industrial or electronic installations nearby to cause interference, and the wall of mountains surrounding the site provided a screen against more distant distractions. So the forest was cleared, a road was blasted through solid ledge, a few acres were bulldozed flat, and the station was built.

There it is, looking like something that Buck Rogers might have dreamed up. For miles and miles about it, the country is still chiefly populated by deer, bear, and bobcats. Some men there still make a part of their living by trapping mink and beaver. Lumberjacks in the area still use two-man crosscut saws to put up their cords of pulpwood, and farmers still turn over the soil with horse-drawn plows. And up in the clearing in the mountains a 210-foot bubble of inflated dacron and synthetic rubber rises weirdly over the forest. Inside it, a gigantic "ear" turns and strains for tiny signals from a twenty-eight inch man-made sphere whirling in outer space. The words from the other side of the world

116

Moosehead Lake, the source of the Kennebec River.

are heard as soon as they are spoken, and the pictures seen as they are being enacted. Yet the signals have traveled at incredible speed millions of miles through the cold and dark of space from earth to Telstar and back to earth again.

But that is the Kennebec. At its source men communicate instantly across thousands of miles of land and sea. At its mouth men go out daily to haul lobster traps. They leave their long-legged wharves when the first flush of dawn creeps up the eastern sky. Each is alone in the small world of his own boat for long hours. He neither sees nor speaks to another human being until he returns to harbor. He is completely out of touch with a world that he can see on the western horizon. The Kennebec is a river of contradictions.

It is a river of variety. It passes through almost every imaginable kind of country and along its course the distant past, the busy present and the exciting future blend so happily that it is hard to tell where one ends and the next begins. It is a river of surprises. Who would dream that up near South Paris, under the fields of blowing timothy grass, there is a whole hill full of semiprecious gems? It is a river that lends itself to hard work, but it lends itself to recreation just as easily.

It is the Kennebec, not quite like any other river in the world.

Index

Abenaki dictionary, Father Râles, 44

Abenakis, the, 17–27, 37, 42, 46–47, 49

attitude of, toward white men, 24, 25, 26

Castin adopted by, 45

government of, 23–24

Abraham, Plains of, 62

agricultural exports, of Maine today, 76

Aix-la-Chapelle, Treaty of, 57

Alden, John, 38

Ames, Colonel Adelbert, 86

Andover, 116

Androscoggin, tributary of the Kennebec, 9–10, 81

exploration of, 29

See also Little Androscoggin

Androscoggin, the first Maine vessel in cotton trade, 75, 115–116

Arnold, Benedict, 42

march of, to Quebec, 58–63

Arrowsic, 49, 51

artifacts, clues provided by, 14–16

Augusta, 37

seat of government moved to, 77

automotive industry, beginning of, 98

Bath, 34, 64–65, 68, 75, 78, 84

first bank in, 76

Baxter, Reverend Joseph, 46

Biddeford, 34

birch, white, uses of, 20–23

blockade, coastal, 72

Blythe, William, 70–72

Boston, Mass., 51, 53, 72

rivalry between Plymouth and, 38

Bowdoin College, 78

Bowdoin Pines, 78

bounty, for scalps and captives, 50

Boxer, the, 69–71

British East India Company, Orient trade controlled by, 67

British rule, colonies' discontent with, 57

Brunswick, 29, 64, 68, 75, 78, 84, 89, 114

Protestant church at, 46

Bull Run, 85, 86

Bunker Hill, 59

Burrows, Lieutenant William, 70–72

Cabot, John, 27
Cabot, Sebastian, 27
Calais, 34
Campobello, 27
canning industry, 110
canoes, 21
Canucks, 114–115
captives, bounty for, 50
Carratunk, graves found at, 14
Cartier, ——, 27
Castin, Jean Vincent de l'Abadie, Baron de, 45–46
Castine, 37
Champlain, Samuel de, 40
Chaudiere River, 42, 58, 59, 61
chewing gum. *See* spruce
China Trade, era of, 67–68
Christmas trees, 110–111
Christmas wreaths, 111
Civil War, 84–90
clipper ships, 67–69
Clough, Captain Samuel, 98–101
cobblestones, 97
Colburn, Major, 59
Columbus, ——, 27
commerce, 66
cotton mill, 75
cotton trade, 76, 84
courage and endurance, legend of Kennebec, 63
coureurs de bois, 40
Courtship of Miles Standish, The, 38
Crockett's Ridge, 104, 105

curse, Molly Ockett's, 88, 89
Cushnoc, 37–41, 59, 77
    meaning of the name, 37
    Protestants of, 42, 44
    See also Fort Western

Damariscotta, 49, 55
Dawn People. *See* Abenakis, the
deer hunting, 113
diet, well-balanced Indian, 18
Dochet Island, French colony on, 34
driftwood, uses of, 98
Druillettes, Father Gabriel, 42–44, 58
duck hunting, 111–113
Dudley, Governor, of Boston, 38
Dunham, Mellie, 104–106

East India Company, British, 67
Embargo Act of 1807, 69
Empress of China, the, 67
English and French, trouble between, 44, 45
Enterprise, the, 69–71
Ericson, Leif, 25
exports from Kennebec region, 97–107
Europeans, first to enter the Kennebec, 17, 24, 25
explorers, 25, 27, 29

Falmouth, burning of, 46
    See also Portland

120

farmers, today's Kennebec Valley, 18, 31, 109–111
  See also Abenakis
Ferdinando, ———, 27
Fiddler, Champion
  of Maine, 104
  old-time, of the U.S., 105
Fish and Game Commission, State Inland, 113
fishermen, 28, 32
Ford, Henry, 104–105
forest, reckless use of, 78–80, 83
Fort Popham, 70
Fort Sumter, 85
Fort Western, 59, 77
  See also Cushnoc
France, attempted rescue of Queen of. *See* Marie Antoinette
French, Canadian Indians' relations with, 40–41
French and English, trouble between, 44–48
French and Indian Wars, 45, 48, 51, 97
French-Canadians, along the Kennebec, 114–115
French in the New World, 34–35, 54
fur trading, 36, 40, 45

Gettysburg, Maine Volunteers at, 86–88
Gibraltar of America. *See* Louisbourg

Gilbert, Raleigh, 29
Gomez, Esteban, 27
Gilbert, Sir Humphrey, 29
Gorges, Sir Fernando, 29, 34
Gosnold, Bartholomew, 29
"Governor, Maine's first and best," 77
Greene, Captain John, 67
guides, hunting, 113

Hallowell, 77, 84
Hamlin, Hannibal, 89
Harding, Nathaniel, 75
Harrington, 77
Hawkins, Sir John, 36
Herringtown, 77
Hocking, ———, murder of, 37–38
Horse Marines, 72
House, Henry Alonzo, steam automobile built by, 98
Howland, John, 37
hunters, 111

ice industry, 91–95
India, search for Northwest Passage to, 27
Indian raids, 49–50
Indians
  Canadian, relations of, with the French, 40–41
  English treatment of, 48, 49
  French treatment of, 48
  See also Abenakis

industries:
  canning, 110
  ice, 91–95
  post-Revolutionary War, 64, 65
inventions, Shaker, 103

Jamestown, Va., 31
Jaquish Island, 47

Katahdin
  first white man to see, 42
  grave clay from, 15
  Spirit of, 23
Kennebec River
  beginning of, 9
  first bridge over, 77
  first settlers on, 13
  first white man on upper, 42
  importance of, 10
  Indian name for, 10
  size of, 9
  tributary of, 9
Kennebec Valley
  bonds of, with the South, 84
  English in, 44
  first settlers in, 13–16
  involvement of, in Civil War, 84
  ruination of, 83
  terror in, 48–57
  today's, 108–118
King, William, 74–77

land grant, 34

language, Kennebec's own, 106–107
Lewiston, 114
Little Androscoggin, 88, 102
  See also Androscoggin
Longfellow (Henry Wadsworth), 38
Long Reach, 64–65
Louisbourg, 54, 57
lumbering, 78–83, 116
  in Viking days, 25

McCobb, Samuel, 59

Machias, trading post at, 37
Maine
  admission of, to the Union, 72
  father of, 29
  first murder to be recorded in, 37–38
  French and Indian Wars spread to, 49
  homesteading in, 32
  importance of Kennebec to state of, 10
  a part of Massachusetts, 36
  statehood for, 74, 76, 77
Maine State Highway 201, 42
Margaretta, the, 70
Marie Antoinette, scheme to rescue, 100–101
marine insurance company, first Maine, 76
marque and reprisal, letters of, 85

122

Massachusetts
  French and Indian Wars begun
    in, 48
  Maine a part of, 36
  separation of Maine from, 72,
    77
masts, 65, 79
Mayflower, 36–37
menhaden, use of, as fertilizer, 17
Merrymeeting Bay, 9, 29, 34, 83
  duck hunting at, 111–113
mission, French, destruction of,
  47
missionaries, Jesuit, 42
  concern of, for Indian converts,
    40
Mr. Madison's War, 72
Monhegan Island, 32, 71
Monmouth, Maine men at, 58
Montcalm, ———, 77
Montgomery, ———, 62
Moosehead, 80
  deer hunting at, 113
  Kennebec begins at, 9
Mud Clipper Fleet, 72
Munjoy Hill, 72
murder, first to be recorded in
  Maine, 37–38

New England, Governor General
  of, 34
Nickerson, Captain Samuel, 113
Norridgewock, 44, 47, 59
  mission at, 42

Norumbega, 27, 28
  colony founded at. *See* Popham
Nova Scotia, 53–54, 56

Ockett, Molly, 88–89
Oxford County, 115
Oyster Shell men, 15, 16

papermaking, 81–83
Peary, Admiral Robert, E., Dun-
  ham snowshoes worn by, 104
Pemaquid, 32, 34, 49, 71
  destruction of, 46
Penobscot River, 34, 45
Pentagoet, 37, 45, 46
Pepperell, William, 55
Philip, King, 48
Phips, William, 51
picking season, 110
Pilgrims, 32, 36–38, 44
pine, Viking need for, 25
Pines, Bowdoin, 78
pines, mast, 65, 79, 80
Piscataqua River, 34
Plymouth, Mass., 36
  rivalry between Boston and, 38
Plymouth Company, 29, 34
Plymouth Rock, 32
Popham, George, 29, 31
Popham, Sir John, 29
Popham, 64
  colony founded at, 29–32
  Fort, 70
  See also Norumbega

popple, 81
Portland, 70, 71
    first state capital, 77
    See also Falmouth
Port Royal, Nova Scotia, 53–54
Pring, Martin, 29
Protestant faith, conversion of
    Indians to, 40–41
pulpwood, 81, 116

Quebec, 48, 57
    Arnold's march to, 42, 58–63
    surrender of, 77
Quinnebequi, Indian name for
    Kennebec, 10

raids, Indian, 49–50
Râle, Father Sebastien, 44, 46–47
Raleigh, Sir Walter, 29
Rangeley Lakes, 80
Red Clay people, 14, 15
Reunion, the, 75
Revolutionary War, 58, 64
Richard Cory (ballad), 106
river-drivers ("river-hogs"), 79
River God, Indian name for Ken-
    nebec, 10
rivers, importance of, 9, 10
Robinson, Edwin Arlington, 106
Rose, the, 53
Rumford, 108, 114

Sabbathday Lake, 102–103
Saco, 34

St. Croix River, 34
Sally, the, 100
Saratoga, Maine men at, 58
Scarboro, boy from. *See* King,
    William
scalps
    bounty for, 50
    trade in, 97
seamen, impressment of Ameri-
    can, 69
seasons along the Kennebec, 13–
    14, 17, 18, 20, 31
    See also weather; winters
settlers
    first, along Kennebec, 13–16, 28
    Maine, 34
Seymour, Richard, 29
Shakers, 102–103
ship, first built by Europeans in
    New World, 32
shipbuilding, 53, 64–65, 75, 78
    See also Masts
Skowhegan, 106, 108
Smith, John, 29
Smith, Margaret Chase, 106
Smithsonian Institution, Dunham
    snowshoes in, 104
smugglers, 69
Snow Falls, Indian curse on, 88,
    89
South, Kennebec Valley ties to
    the, 84–85
Spencer, Captain Roger, 51

spruce, 80–81
Standish, Miles, 38
State Inland Fish and Game Commission, 113
Stillwater, Maine men at, 58
stockades, 49
Stowe, Harriet Beecher, 89–90
Sumter, Fort, 85
Swanton, William, 64

Telstar Earth Station, first, at Andover, 116–118
territorial claims, early, 27
Ticonderoga, Maine men at, 58
today's Kennebec, 108–118
Topsham, 74–75, 77
tourism, 113–114
trading posts, 36, 37
    French, at Pentagoet, 45
treasure, finding lost, 53
Twentieth Maine, the, 86–88

Uncle Tom's Cabin, 90

Vacationland, 113
Valley Forge, Maine men at, 58
Vaughn, Louis, 55

Vikings, 25, 27
Virginia of Sagadahoc, 32, 64

Walker, John, 27
Wampanoag, 48
Wars:
    Civil, 84–90
    Eighteen Twelve, 72, 77
    French and Indian, 45, 48, 51, 97
    Mr. Madison's, 64–73
    Revolutionary, 58, 64
Washington, George, 58
Waterville, 114
weather, industrial importance of, 31, 56, 79, 92–95
    See also seasons along the Kennebec; winters
Westbrook, Captain, 47
Western, Fort, 77
West Indies trade, 53, 65
Weymouth, George, 29
Winslow, John, 44
winters, 31, 60
winter sports, 93–94
Wiscasset, 68, 98, 100, 101
Wolfe, ———, 57
Wolfe's Cove, 62
Woolwich, 49, 51